GOBBA GOBBA HEY

GABBA, GABBA.

WE ACCEPT YOU,

WE ACCEPT YOU ONE OF US!

—THE RAMONES

GOBBA GOBBA HEY

A gob cook- book

STEVEN GDULA

BLOOMSBURY

NEW YORK · BERLIN · LONDON · SYDNEY

PUBLISHED BY Bloomsbury USA, New York

All papers used by Bloomsbury USA are natural, recyclable products made from wood grown in well-managed forests. The manufacturing processes conform to the environmental regulations of the country of origin.

LIBRARY OF CONGRESS CATALOGING-IN-PUBLICATION DATA
Gdula, Steven.
Gobba Gobba Hey : a gob cookbook / Steven Gdula.—1st U.S. ed.
p. cm.
Includes index.
ISBN-13: 978-1-60819-478-0 (hardback)
ISBN-10: 1-60819-478-7 (hardback)
1. Whoopie pies. 2. Gobba Gobba Hey (Bakery) 3. Cookbooks. I. Title.
TX772.G39 2011
641.8'15—dc22   2011000277

First U.S. Edition 2011

1 9 8 7 6 5 4 3 2 1

Printed in the U.S.A. by Quad/Graphics, Fairfield, Pennsylvania

FOR MY PARENTS, WHOSE D.I.Y. KITCHEN TAUGHT ME MOST OF WHAT I KNOW . . .

. . . IN MEMORY OF MY DAD.

CONTENTS

TRODUCTION

"Do I want to buy a what? A gob? What's a gob?"

The question caught me off guard. The woman standing in front of me was my first potential customer, and I was about to lose her.

What's a gob? What's a gob!? Doesn't everyone know what a gob is? I wondered, a little panicked.

I reached into my cooler for one of the confections I'd baked just a few hours earlier, as my mind raced to find the right words to describe what I thought was one of the most delicious of all the guilty pleasures I'd ever had. "This is a gob," I said, smiling hopefully as I handed her one of my plastic-wrapped treats to inspect. She immediately lifted it to her nose to get a whiff of the alluring aromas of ginger, orange, and cardamom. She nodded her head approvingly and closed her eyes. She sniffed again.

"Mmmm. It smells incredible. But what *is* it?" she asked, now more curious than ever. She craned her neck to see what else might be in my cooler.

"A gob is, well, it's a . . . " I took a deep breath and launched into my pitch.

A gob, I explained, is a beguiling little treat that you find back east, especially in parts of Pennsylvania. Made of two domes of moist, dense cake with filling in the middle, a gob is kind of like a cupcake sandwich. But without any crumbs. They're usually chocolate cake with vanilla filling. "But the one you're holding now," I told her, "has grated organic ginger, fresh orange, and cardamom baked in the batter, while the filling is buttercream whipped with a saffron-infused syrup that I made."

"It smells so *good*," she said.

The gob was once again back up in front of her face. But . . . was she going to buy it? Was she going to hand it back, wish me luck, and continue on her way?

Nervously, I stepped up my pitch. "You've never eaten a gob before?" I asked. "Well, back east we eat them all the time. In my neck of the woods, they are everywhere. You can find them in commercial bakeries, at community bake sales, picnics, birthday parties, car wash fund-raisers, and even gas stations. Some people say their origins are Pennsylvania Dutch—"

"So, is this, like, street food?" the woman interrupted.

"Yes, in a manner of speaking, I suppose you could say that it is."

She opened her purse, pulled out her wallet, and asked, "How much?"

With that, I had made my first sale, and my customer had her first gob. As she walked away, a few more interested parties gathered around.

"Whatcha got?"

"What flavors do you have?"

"What are they called again?"

And of course, I also received the uniquely San Franciscan request: "Do you have any that are *special*?"

What was going on here? I didn't have time to ponder it long, as a few more passersby slowed their pace to ask what I was selling. Some people bought one. Some bought two. Some didn't buy at all. But everyone asked questions, and everyone wished me luck.

At some point, in between my reaching into the cooler for a gob and handing it to my next customer, a line had formed. A very small line, but a line just the same. The interest amazed me, but it was my customers' appreciation of my plight and their understanding of the reason for my street sales that really touched me. When asked what had brought me out onto the street that day, I explained that I was underemployed and looking for a way to make ends meet. The afternoon passed, and at least two people who had bought from me earlier that day circled back, returning from their errands.

"Those were delicious!" they said. "Where can we find you again?"

I was momentarily stumped. Just as the

previous "what's a gob?" query had taken me aback, so did the question regarding future sales. I hadn't really been banking on this as a long-term business plan.

Before I could answer, a woman came up with another question that would prove to be a game changer: "Do you tweet?"

I did, but I didn't. I had established a Twitter account because experts insisted it was necessary for self-promotion in these uncertain financial times, but I honestly didn't know how to use it. I opted for the affirmative half-truth. "Yep," I replied, "I'm on Twitter."

"Great! I'll '@' you," the woman said. At least I knew what that meant—she would reference me in her own feed. With that, she walked away with a wave.

I got home that evening, logged onto Twitter, and saw to my astonishment that I had developed a small following. Several of my customers from that afternoon were already tweeting about my gobs. The next day I got a call from Tamara Palmer, a food columnist for *SF Weekly*, asking if she could sample my wares. She said she'd read about my gobs online. People were talking. And I was speechless.

I had left the house that first day with a supply of four dozen gobs—half of them Orange, Cardamom, Ginger with Saffron Filling and the other half Carrot Cake with Citrus Cream Cheese Filling. In an hour's time, I had sold more than a dozen of each.

Now, I knew my day's sales—at a dollar per gob—weren't going to right my economic world any time soon, but as far as I was concerned, the outing was a success. The fact that I had more money in my pocket when I returned to my house than I'd had when I left was proof enough. And anyway, I wasn't counting my good fortune in terms of dollars and cents. I was calculating in a currency that was more abstract but every bit as valuable to me.

The truth is that on that Sunday afternoon when I took to the streets of San Francisco's Mission District with my homemade gobs, I had been looking for the same thing that millions of other Americans were also looking for in the spring of 2009: a job. But I was also looking for a sense of purpose. A freelance writer for most of my adult life, I had found myself all but out of work, with weeks going by without a single writing assignment.

Compounding the lack of stability in my life was the unanticipated period of adjustment to San Francisco, my new hometown. A lifelong East Coast resident, I had longed to move west since my first visit to the Bay Area in the early 1990s. In October 2008 I had made that dream a reality, but with real estate prices what they were, the only house my spouse and I could afford was a fixer-upper—and it was proving to be a real downer. The windows leaked, the floors sagged, and the exterior would've given Boo Radley a chill. But it was the disrepair of the kitchen that was, for me, a lifelong cooking enthusiast, the most dispiriting. Outdated appliances and years of neglect made the room less than welcoming. Ironically, my last substantial paycheck had been for a book I'd written about kitchens, *The Warmest Room in the House*, celebrating the room's role at the center of the American home. But, as I'd concluded in my cultural history, while technological advances and modern appliances have made today's kitchens convenient, it has always been a family's history and traditions that make the room truly inviting.

So, lacking funds for an immediate renovation, I relied instead on cooking comfort foods from my past to transform the dilapidated scullery of our current home into the warmest room in our house. In an attempt to remind myself of who I was in this new place, I cooked my way through the recipes that had comforted me over the years and helped shape my identity inside, and outside, of the kitchen. Lacking other work, I had a lot of time to perfect those recipes. I browned chicken on top of the stove for my ancestral chicken paprikash. I slid my take on macaroni and cheese—penne, heavy cream, and oozing amounts of Gruyère and cheddar—into the oven. And, reaching way back in my memory for a long-shelved recipe, I began baking gobs.

As I was hunkering down in my San Francisco kitchen, some intrepid souls were stepping out of theirs. On a small side street in the city's Mission District, two brothers were serving their friends and neighbors Thai curry and crème brûlée from homemade, curbside carts. Brian and Curtis Kimball modeled their Magic Curry Kart and Crème Brûlée Cart, respectively, after the informal street food vendors who sell small dishes and concessions in cities around the world.

The streets of San Francisco's Mission District have long been home to several taco vendors peddling their delicious and authentic wares from trucks—as well as the beloved Tamale Lady, who sells her wares from a cooler. But the emergence of vendors selling foods that weren't always associated with street food, such as crème brûlée, was something new in the spring of 2009. Operating without proper licenses, these new purveyors were, in most cases, underemployed in their given fields and were gingerly referred to in the press as "independent" or "nontraditional." By the time I was inspired to joined their ranks with my cooler full of gobs, about a half-dozen similar carts had rolled onto the city's streets. There were cookie bakers (Cookie Wag), hand-squeezed juice artisans (Urban Nectar), pie makers (Bike Basket Pies), pastry chefs (Amuse Bouche), vegan bakers (Wholesome Bakery), and organic, vegetarian soup ladlers (Sexy Soup Cart). The do-it-yourself ethic of it all gave the new street vendor scene a punk feel. Few of us were professionally trained, beyond having slung hash or worked as a line or a grill cook at some point in our lives. But what we lacked in formal culinary education, we made up for in passion and enthusiasm, as well as a strong commitment to the dishes from our individual pasts that we were now selling on the street. A community was quickly being built, and with it, a small but unique type of local economy.

I found myself a part of this growing scene through what I can refer to only as one of the happiest of accidents. San Francisco is a food-obsessed city with a lot of food-focused publications and Web sites, and as I was scrolling through readers' comments on Chow.com, looking for ideas for food stories to pitch, a single message caught my eye: A regular user on the site had posted that San Francisco's new fleet of street carts "were *coordinating!*" The breathless excitement of this single expression was contagious. I wanted to know more. I started researching online and I soon decided I didn't just want to cover this nascent street cart movement as a journalist; I wanted to join it.

But what could I contribute? I was quite literally the new kid on the block, and I didn't want to step on any toes or invade anyone's turf. But the answer was easy—it could be read in the dirty mixing bowls and baking sheets accumulating in my sink. In my months in San Francisco, I had never seen a gob or its counterpart, the whoopie pie—a similar pastry, with a marshmallow-based filling in contrast to the gob's cream cheese or buttercream middle—anywhere outside my kitchen. My mind was set. I would take my gobs to the streets.

For almost six weeks after first reading that Chow.com post, I worked on perfecting gob recipes in my home kitchen. The Original Chocolate and Vanilla Gob was my sentimental favorite, and while I knew that well-executed classics are always appreciated, here in the "new food capital of the world," I felt I needed to bring some excitement to my game. The local farmer's markets, whose rows of bright greens and seasonal fruits had already provided me with hours of wonderment, now helped inform my new baking venture. Neighbors and new friends were the tasters for gob flavor combinations such as Carrot Cake with Citrus Cream Cheese Filling; "Black Cherry" with Lime Buttercream Filling; and the now-

infamous Chocolate-Fennel with Raspberry Absinthe.

As my confidence in my baking skills grew, so did my attachment to my run-down kitchen. I now looked forward to spending hours surrounded by its shabby cabinets and dull tiles. After long neglect, this kitchen was producing a confection that made people smile at first bite.

Now my new venture needed a name. Taking a cue from another fave from my youth—the Ramones song "Pinhead," with its refrain of "Gabba Gabba Hey!"—I christened it Gobba Gobba Hey. Without the means to rent or build a real cart, I had to start humbly. I purchased a plastic serving tray from Target, a cooler from Costco, and some stickers from Office Depot. I baked and frosted the gobs on a Sunday morning, covered them in plastic wrap, sealed each one with a Gobba Gobba Hey sticker, and put them in the fridge to allow them to set and the flavors to meld. Several hours later I was standing on a well-trafficked sidewalk in the Mission.

After that first day of introducing passersby to the concept of the gob—and gaining a Twitter following overnight—

business was swift. Within a month of my curbside debut, I was selling gobs at the farmer's market at San Francisco's hallowed food hall, the Ferry Building. A month after that, I moved my operations into a commercial kitchen (as much as I now loved my own, it had only one oven) and was looking into wholesaling to retail stores. People were ordering gobs by the dozens for their client meetings, birthday parties, weekend-long food festivals, and even weddings. Local grocery stores as well as large national chains expressed interest in carrying Gobba Gobba Hey gobs. Some of the media outlets that I had once pitched stories to were now covering my gobs as part of the San Francisco street food phenomenon. Gobba Gobba Hey popped up on lists of "must-haves" and "top foods to try" for visitors to the city.

People often ask if I'd ever imagined that Gobba Gobba Hey would come this far. Honestly? No. I thought it would be a way to supplement my income—maybe make some good connections in the food community, meet people who might hire me to write in the future. That ploy worked to some extent, but in an almost comical twist, my baking responsibilities now prevent me from taking on many writing assignments. Gob duties even slowed down the completion of this cookbook!

It's been almost two years since I first took my gobs out my front door and onto the streets of San Francisco. Most of the recipes contained here have been offered somewhere in the city at one point or another. A few have been baked solely for friends, and a very select few have been baked for friends' birthday parties. I hope you will have as much fun making them as I have, but even more fun eating them and sharing them with others.

These recipes helped me find my place in my new kitchen and in my new hometown. I hope you will give them a welcome place in yours.

AUTHOR'S NOTE

This book contains fifty-two recipes, one for every week of the year. The recipes are arranged more or less as I developed them throughout the course of my first gob-baking year. Often times I allowed the local farmer's markets to inspire my recipes. Other times I defaulted to the offerings of my local grocery store when I couldn't peruse the bins and stalls of the outdoor markets. My year began in mid-spring and ended in winter, so many of the gobs follow the seasonal availability of ingredients at the San Francisco farmer's markets.

Each recipe in this book is unique, tested, and tweaked to make the most of the flavor combinations. Depending on how generous your scoop, each recipe should yield approximately thirty complete gobs. A standup mixer with a paddle attachment will work best with these recipes, but if you have a hand mixer, that will work as well. The syrups will provide you with enough for at least two batches of filling. You can use any additional syrup for drizzling over your favorite ice cream or stirring into your alcohol of choice for a delicious cocktail! The syrups will last for two weeks if stored in an airtight container in your fridge. The gobs will keep, tightly covered and refrigerated, for a week to ten days. You can also freeze them. Just make sure you use a secure Ziploc-style bag.

I've been told by many of Gobba Gobba Hey's customers that they prefer bringing the gobs to room temperature before enjoying. This is a matter of choice, obviously.

No matter which gob you choose, you'll find the process is quite simple: Each recipe includes directions for batter (for the gob "domes"), for the pulp that provides the flavor, when appropriate, and also for the syrups that make each filling so delicious!

I hope that the gobs provide endless enjoyment, as they have for me, and that they also provide inspiration for your own experimentation. Bake—and enjoy!

ORIGINAL CHOCOLATE & VANILLA GOBS

"There's history in every kitchen." I'd written that line in the introduction to my last book, *The Warmest Room in the House*, and it came to mind often as I was trying to make a fixer-upper in my new hometown feel more like home. The kitchen seemed like the best place to start.

The room had plenty of history—evident in the grime gumming the appliances—but that history wasn't mine. I cleaned out cupboards and relined drawers. I unpacked boxes and found places for my favorite cookbooks, cutlery, and pots and pans. We settled in, but despite the familiarity of my battery and my favorite recipes, I still longed for a taste of home.

In thinking about the comforting foods from my past, I found the solution. I decided to bake gobs. I wanted to revisit the deep bewitchingly dark chocolate color and moistness of the cake. I longed for the white and fluffy and cloyingly sweet filling. I wanted to wrap each one in plastic wrap just so I could giddily unwrap it later and run my finger along the chocolate imprint left on the plastic.

This is the recipe, handed down from my parents, for the first batch of gobs I ever baked. Chocolate and vanilla is the classic combination that started it all.

1. Preheat the oven to 350°F. Line three 8-by-13-inch cookie sheets with parchment paper.

2. In a large bowl, sift together the flour, cocoa powder, baking powder, baking soda, and salt. Whisk the dry ingredients thoroughly.

3. In another large bowl, cream together the sugar and vegetable shortening with a mixer on medium speed. Add the eggs and vanilla to the creamed ingredients, and blend on medium-high until the mixture looks like dense pudding.

4. Alternate adding the dry ingredients and the buttermilk to the egg mixture, mixing on medium speed after each addition. Mix well. Add water as needed to thin the batter. ("Go lightly" was my mom's original instruction.)

5. Using a tablespoon or a pastry bag, drop 1½-inch rounds of batter on the prepared cookie sheets, leaving 1 inch between each round. Bake them approximately 8 minutes, or until the gob domes have risen. Remove the gobs to a wire rack to cool.

1. Heat the milk in a saucepan over low heat. Bring to simmer and immediately add the flour. Whisk. Continue mixing over low heat til mixture thickens, approximately 3 to 5 minutes. Remove and allow to cool.

2. With a mixer on medium speed, cream together the vegetable shortening and margarine. Add the vanilla and sugar, and mix on medium-high.

3. Add the cooled milk-flour mixture to the creamed ingredients, and beat until the mixture is fluffy; scrape the bowl with a spatula to reincorporate the ingredients if necessary.

4. To frost the gobs, flip the baked gob domes over on a cookie sheet and match up pairs of similarly shaped domes. Add 1 tablespoon of filling to the flat side of an overturned dome, then place another dome on top, sandwich-style. Allow the gobs to fully set by refrigerating them on a baking sheet for at least 1 hour. Wrap the gobs in plastic wrap to prevent them from drying out.

FOR THE **BATTER**

- 4 cups all-purpose FLOUR
- ¾ cup COCOA POWDER
- ½ teaspoon BAKING POWDER
- 2 teaspoons BAKING SODA
- 1 teaspoon SALT
- ½ cup VEGETABLE SHORTENING, such as Crisco
- 2 cups SUGAR, sifted
- 2 EGGS, at room temperature
- 1 teaspoon VANILLA EXTRACT
- 1 cup BUTTERMILK, at room temperature
- 1 cup WATER, or as needed

FOR THE **FILLING**

- 1 cup MILK
- 4 tablespoons all-purpose FLOUR
- ½ cup VEGETABLE SHORTENING, such as Crisco
- ½ cup MARGARINE
- 1 teaspoon VANILLA EXTRACT
- 1 cup GRANULATED SUGAR, or 2 cups confectioners' sugar, sifted

S.F. CHOCOLATE VANILLA GOB

Vegetable shortening has never been a staple in my kitchen. My parents' gob recipe calls for it, but I wanted to try swapping it out for butter. I did have a nagging concern about making that switch: Would an all-dairy gob lose the confection's characteristic moistness?

My answer came with the first buttery batch I baked. The gobs are still every bit as tantalizing in texture as the ones made with vegetable shortening.

I overhauled the filling recipe, too. When made with butter, the gob filling has a wholly different, creamier mouthfeel. With a little tweaking I created a butter-based gob filling that I like to call "fresh-whipped sin." The warm vanilla flavor is nicely tinged with a little lemon. For the batter, I like Green & Black's organic cocoa powder. Its smoky, almost espresso-like richness is perfect with the cool, tangy filling.

1. Preheat the oven to 350°F. Line three 8-by-13-inch cookie sheets with parchment paper.

2. In a large bowl, sift together the flour, cocoa powder, baking powder, baking soda, and salt. Whisk the dry ingredients until they're evenly distributed.

3. In another large bowl, cream together the sugar and butter with a mixer on medium speed. Add the egg yolks to the creamed ingredients, and mix on medium. Then add the egg whites and vanilla, and mix on medium-high until the mixture looks like dense pudding.

4. Alternate adding the dry ingredients and the buttermilk to the egg mixture, mixing on medium speed after each addition. Then add the sour cream, and mix well. (If batter is too thick add additional buttermilk, one tablespoon at a time, mixing well after each, until smooth.)

5. Using a tablespoon or a pastry bag, drop 1½-inch rounds of batter on the prepared cookie sheets, leaving 1 inch between each round. Bake them approximately 8 minutes, or until the gob domes have risen. Remove the gobs to a wire rack to cool.

1. Cream together the butter and cream cheese with a mixer on medium speed.

2. Add the vanilla, confectioners' sugar, sour cream, and 1 tablespoon of lemon juice, and beat on high speed until peaks form; scrape the bowl with a spatula to reincorporate the ingredients if necessary. Taste and add another tablespoon of lemon juice if you like.

3. To frost the gobs, flip the baked gob domes over on a cookie sheet and match up pairs of similarly shaped domes. Add 1 tablespoon of filling to the flat side of an overturned dome, then place another dome on top, sandwich-style. Allow the gobs to fully set by refrigerating them on a baking sheet for at least 1 hour. Wrap the gobs in plastic wrap to prevent them from drying out.

FOR THE BATTER

- **4 cups all-purpose FLOUR**
- **½ cup COCOA POWDER**
- **½ teaspoon BAKING POWDER**
- **1½ teaspoons BAKING SODA**
- **1 teaspoon SALT**
- **2 cups SUGAR, sifted**
- **8 tablespoons UNSALTED BUTTER, softened, cut in ½-inch cubes**
- **2 EGGS, separated, at room temperature**
- **1 teaspoon VANILLA EXTRACT**
- **1 cup BUTTERMILK, at room temperature**
- **2 tablespoons SOUR CREAM**

FOR THE FILLING

- **8 TABLESPOONS UNSALTED BUTTER, softened, cut in ½-inch cubes**
- **12 tablespoons CREAM CHEESE, cut in ½-inch cubes**
- **2 tablespoons SOUR CREAM**
- **2 tablespoons plus 1 teaspoon VANILLA EXTRACT**
- **2 cups CONFECTIONERS' SUGAR, sifted**
- **1 to 2 tablespoons fresh LEMON JUICE**

ORANGE, CARDAMOM, Ginger Gobs WITH Saffron FILLING

If I had to pick a gob flavor that inspired all the others that have emerged from my kitchen, this would be it. Once this recipe's bronze-hued and aromatic domes came out of the oven, my newly acquired interest in baking went from weekend dabbling to a daily habit. Ladies and gentlemen, these were the gateway gobs.

I adapted this recipe from an old cake recipe. Friends have always referred to me as one of those "instinctual cooks," and I suppose it's true. I know how to improvise salad dressings and marinades, appetizers, and entrées, but baking, with its reliance on precise measurements and processes, always seemed daunting. As I saw it, if I could successfully manipulate these flavors into a new gob recipe, then I was only bound by the limits of my imagination. And, of course, my larder.

The Orange, Cardamom, Ginger Gobs with Saffron Filling were an immediate hit among my original taste testers, and I was on my way. The fresh-grated ginger and orange zest in the recipe not only add to this gob's intoxicating aroma; they also help moisten the cake.

1. Preheat the oven to 350°F. Line three 8-by-13-inch cookie sheets with parchment paper.

2. In a large bowl, sift together the flour, cardamom, baking powder, baking soda, and salt. Whisk the dry ingredients until they're evenly distributed.

3. In another large bowl, cream together the sugar and butter with a mixer on medium speed. Add the yolks to the creamed ingredients and mix on high. Add the egg whites and vanilla to the creamed ingredients, and blend on medium-high speed until the mixture looks like dense pudding. Then add the grated ginger and orange zest, and beat on high speed until they're incorporated.

4. Alternate adding the dry ingredients and the buttermilk to the egg mixture, mixing on medium speed after each addition. Then add the sour cream, and mix well.

5. Using a tablespoon or pastry bag, drop 1½-inch rounds of batter on the prepared cookie sheets, leaving 1 inch between each round. Bake them approximately 8 minutes, or until the gob domes have risen. Remove the gobs to wire rack to cool.

FOR THE BATTER

- 4 cups plus 2 tablespoons all-purpose FLOUR
- 3 tablespoons GROUND CARDAMOM
- ½ teaspoon BAKING POWDER
- 1½ teaspoons BAKING SODA
- 1 teaspoon SALT
- 2 cups SUGAR, sifted
- 8 tablespoons UNSALTED BUTTER, softened, cut in ½-inch cubes
- 2 EGGS, separated, at room temperature
- 1 teaspoon VANILLA EXTRACT
- 1½ tablespoons grated fresh GINGER
- 2 tablespoons ORANGE ZEST
- 1 cup BUTTERMILK, at room temperature
- 2 tablespoons SOUR CREAM

1. Cream together the butter and cream cheese with a mixer on medium speed.

2. Add the vanilla, 1 tablespoon of lemon juice, 3 tablespoons of saffron syrup, and the confectioners' sugar, and beat on medium-high speed; scrape the bowl with a spatula if necessary to reincorporate the ingredients. Taste and add another tablespoon of lemon juice or saffron syrup if you like.

3. To frost the gobs, flip the baked gob domes over on a cookie sheet and match up pairs of similarly shaped domes. Add 1 tablespoon of filling to the flat side of an overturned dome, then place another dome on top, sandwich-style. Allow the gobs to fully set by refrigerating them on a baking sheet for at least 1 hour. Wrap the gobs in plastic wrap to prevent them from drying out.

FOR THE FILLING

- 8 tablespoons UNSALTED BUTTER, softened, cut in ½-inch cubes
- 12 tablespoons CREAM CHEESE, cut in ½-inch cubes
- 1 teaspoon VANILLA EXTRACT
- 1 to 2 tablespoons fresh LEMON JUICE
- 3 to 4 tablespoons SAFFRON SYRUP (recipe follows)
- 2 cups CONFECTIONERS' SUGAR, sifted

1. Place the sugar, orange juice, ginger, saffron, and water in a saucepan. Bring the liquid to a boil over medium heat, stirring to dissolve the sugar.

2. Reduce the heat to low and simmer, stirring occasionally, until the mixture reduces by half (about 15 minutes).

3. Add the lemon juice to the syrup and mix it well. Remove the pan from the heat and set it aside, covered, to let the syrup steep for at least 20 minutes.

4. Strain into a bowl, reserving the syrup for the gob filling. The syrup will keep, tightly covered, in the fridge for up to 2 weeks.

FOR THE

SAFFRON SYRUP

- 1 cup SUGAR
- 2 cups fresh-squeezed ORANGE JUICE
- 1 tablespoon minced fresh GINGER
- 1½ teaspoons SAFFRON threads, crumbled
- ½ cup WATER
- Juice of 1 LEMON

Lemon-Thyme GOBS

My adventures in gob baking happened to coincide with my experimental phase in cocktail mixology. In bars and restaurants around the Bay Area, I had tasted some dazzling libations that seemed the result of equal parts alchemy and culinary expertise.

Inspired by these drinks, I began steeping herbs, zesting citrus peels, and extracting juices to create a small pantry's worth of syrups and tinctures for cocktails at home. My lemon-thyme reduction was originally intended for a vodka concoction, but as the swizzle stirred, the gears turned, and I imagined a gob batter and filling flavored with this same syrup.

Bundles of thyme were available at the market, and with my new neighbors offering lemons grown in their backyard, I had no shortage of ingredients. Lemon zest adds such a clean, bright flavor to these gobs, and the fresh thyme leaves provide the perfect earthy counterbalance.

RECIPE CONTINUES

1. Preheat the oven to 350°F. Line three 8-by-13-inch baking sheets with parchment paper.

2. In a large bowl, sift together the flour, baking powder, baking soda, and salt. Whisk the dry ingredients until they're evenly distributed.

3. In another large bowl, cream the sugar and butter with a mixer on medium speed. Add the egg yolks to the creamed ingredients, and mix on medium. Then add the egg whites and vanilla, and mix on medium-high until the mixture looks like dense pudding. Add the lemon zest and thyme leaves and mix on high speed until they're incorporated.

4. Alternate adding the dry ingredients and the buttermilk to the egg mixture, mixing on medium speed after each addition. Then add the sour cream, and mix well.

5. Using a tablespoon or a pastry bag, drop 1½-inch rounds of batter on the prepared cookie sheets, leaving 1 inch between each round. Bake them approximately 8 minutes, or until the gob domes have risen. Remove the gobs to a wire rack to cool.

FOR THE BATTER

- 4½ cups all-purpose FLOUR
- ½ teaspoon BAKING POWDER
- 1½ teaspoons BAKING SODA
- 1 teaspoon SALT
- 2 cups SUGAR, sifted
- 8 tablespoons UNSALTED BUTTER, softened, cut in ½-inch cubes
- 2 EGGS, separated, at room temperature
- 1 teaspoon VANILLA EXTRACT
- 2 tablespoons fresh LEMON ZEST
- 1 tablespoon fresh THYME leaves
- 1 cup BUTTERMILK, at room temperature
- 1 tablespoon SOUR CREAM

1. Cream together the butter and cream cheese with a mixer on medium speed.

2. Add the vanilla, 3 tablespoons of the lemon-thyme syrup, and the confectioners' sugar, and beat on medium-high; scrape the bowl with a spatula if necessary to reincorporate the ingredients. Taste and add another tablespoon of lemon-thyme syrup if you like.

3. To frost the gobs, flip the baked gob domes over on a cookie sheet and match up pairs of similarly shaped domes. Add 1 tablespoon of filling to the flat side of a dome, then place another dome on top, sandwich-style. Allow the gobs to fully set by refrigerating them on a baking sheet for at least 1 hour. Wrap the gobs in plastic wrap to prevent them from drying out.

FOR THE FILLING

- 8 tablespoons UNSALTED BUTTER, softened, cut in ½-inch cubes
- 12 tablespoons CREAM CHEESE, cut in ½-inch cubes
- 1 teaspoon VANILLA EXTRACT
- 3 to 4 tablespoons LEMON-THYME SYRUP (recipe follows)
- 2 cups CONFECTIONERS' SUGAR, sifted

1. Place the sugar, lemon juice, thyme sprigs, and water in a saucepan. Bring the liquid to a boil over medium heat, stirring to dissolve the sugar.

2. Reduce the heat to low and simmer, stirring occasionally, until the mixture reduces by about half (about 15 minutes).

3. Remove the pan from the heat and set it aside, covered, to let the syrup steep for at least 20 minutes.

4. Remove the thyme stems and strain the mixture, reserving the syrup for the gob filling. The syrup will keep, tightly covered, in a fridge for up to 2 weeks.

FOR THE

LEMON-THYME SYRUP

1 cup **SUGAR**

JUICE of 3 **LEMONS** (approximately 1 cup)

5 to 7 **THYME** sprigs, leaves intact

½ cup **WATER**

"BLACK CHERRY"

WITH Lime Buttercream FILLING

Cherries had just started to come into season at the farmer's market, and as I eyed their beautiful deep reddish and purple orbs one late spring morning, I was excited about the possibilities. Black cherry was one of my favorite flavors of soda when I was growing up, so the stone fruits were already awakening nostalgia.

I scooped some into a bag, brought them home, and set out to create a black cherry gob. What I didn't realize was that these cherries, which ran from a patent leather red to a deep, merlot burgundy, were not the "black cherries" of my childhood soda fantasies at all. They were Bing cherries. Real black cherries didn't come into season until late summer. On the other side of the country.

But I didn't get too dispirited, and I figured there wasn't anything literally black or sylvan about Black Forest cake other than the regional reference in the name, so I went ahead and called my creations Black Cherry Gobs anyway. Cherries and chocolate make a winsome pair in the batter, and the clean citrus flavor of lime adds the perfect high note to the sexy vanilla and cherry in the filling.

1. Preheat the oven to 350°F. Line three 8-by-13-inch cookie sheets with parchment paper.

2. In a large bowl, sift together the flour, cocoa powder, baking powder, baking soda, and salt. Whisk the dry ingredients until they're evenly distributed.

3. In another large bowl, cream the sugar and butter with a mixer on medium speed. Add the eggs yolks to the mixer bowl, and mix on medium. Add the egg whites and vanilla, and increase the speed to medium-high until the egg mixture looks like dense pudding. Then add the reserved cherries, and beat on high.

4. Alternate adding the dry ingredients and the buttermilk to the egg mixture, mixing on medium speed after each addition. Then add the sour cream, and mix well.

5. Using a tablespoon or a pastry bag, drop 1½-inch rounds of batter on the prepared cookie sheets, leaving 1 inch between each round. Bake them approximately 8 minutes, or until the gob domes have risen. Remove the gobs to a wire rack to cool.

FOR THE **BATTER**

- **4 cups all-purpose FLOUR**
- **½ cup COCOA POWDER (preferably Green & Black's organic)**
- **½ teaspoon BAKING POWDER**
- **1½ teaspoons BAKING SODA**
- **1 teaspoon SALT**
- **2 cups SUGAR, sifted**
- **8 tablespoons UNSALTED BUTTER, softened, cut in ½-inch cubes**
- **2 EGGS, separated, at room temperature**
- **1 teaspoon VANILLA EXTRACT**
- **¼ cup reserved CHERRIES from cherry syrup (recipe follows)**
- **1 cup BUTTERMILK, at room temperature**
- **2 tablespoons SOUR CREAM**

1. Cream together the butter and cream cheese with a mixer on medium speed.

2. Add the vanilla, 1 tablespoon of lime juice, 3 tablespoons of cherry syrup, and the confectioners' sugar, and beat on medium-high; scrape the bowl with a spatula if necessary to reincorporate the ingredients. Taste and add more lime juice or cherry syrup to your taste if you'd like.

3. To frost the gobs, flip the baked gob domes over on a cookie sheet and match up pairs of similarly shaped domes. Add 1 tablespoon of filling to the flat side of an overturned dome, then place another dome on top, sandwich-style. Allow the gobs to fully set by refrigerating them on a baking sheet for at least 1 hour. Wrap the gobs in plastic wrap to prevent them from drying out.

FOR THE **FILLING**

- **8 tablespoons UNSALTED BUTTER, softened, cut in ½-inch cubes**
- **12 tablespoons CREAM CHEESE, cut in ½-inch cubes**
- **1 teaspoon VANILLA EXTRACT**
- **1 to 2 tablespoons fresh LIME JUICE, pulp removed**
- **3 to 4 tablespoons CHERRY SYRUP (recipe follows)**
- **2 cups CONFECTIONERS' SUGAR, sifted**

1. Place the sugar, cherries, vanilla bean, ginger, and water in a saucepan. Bring the liquid to a boil over medium heat, stirring to dissolve the sugar.

2. Reduce the heat to low, and simmer, stirring occasionally, until the mixture reduces by about half (about 15 minutes).

3. Add the lemon juice to the syrup, and stir well. Remove the pan from the heat and set it aside, covered, to let the syrup steep for at least 20 minutes.

4. Remove the vanilla bean and ginger. Strain the cherries from the syrup, reserving the cherries for the gob batter and the syrup for the gob filling; press the cherries to extract as much liquid as possible. The syrup will keep, tightly covered, in a fridge for up to 2 weeks.

FOR THE

CHERRY SYRUP

1 cup **SUGAR**

2 cups fresh **BING CHERRIES**, coarsely chopped, pits removed

1 **VANILLA BEAN**, split, seeds scraped and reserved

1 one-inch piece fresh **GINGER**, sliced into four thick rounds

½ cup **WATER**

2 teaspoons fresh **LEMON JUICE**

PEACHES 'N' CREAM 'N' BOURBON GOBS

When I was growing up, a peach was a peach was a peach. Truth be told, I never got close enough to discern any differences in the fruit anyway, and for one very simple reason: For me, the feel of the fuzzy peel against my teeth created a chill-inducing visceral reaction —the food version of fingernails on a chalkboard.

So it was with steely resolve that I bravely plucked a creamy white-skinned peach from a basket at the farmer's market. Calling a peach "sexy" is as much of a cliché as saying that a steak is "mouthwatering," but as we know, clichés exist for a reason. There's generally truth to them. Looking at the variety of peaches in front of me, I was suddenly aware of a seductive allure I'd never noticed before. I *wanted* to touch them. These peaches were more than just sexy. They were naughty. *Spankable.* The few visible bruises on their skins looked like lipstick, smudged in a hasty kiss.

How had I missed out on this whole peach cult thing before? I was getting a little buzzed by their fragrance. Even the bees swarming overhead seemed to swoop and swerve drunkenly. Slices of the peach varieties on offer sat in bowls for tasting. I was all in. I lifted the slices to my nose in turn and took a whiff. One was crisp and bright, almost citrusy, kind of like a pinot gris. Another was floral. Another smelled of warm honey and bourbon. Oh, to be a bee! My decision was made.

I tossed some of the honey-bourbon-ish peaches into my bag and headed home to bake gobs. A reduction of peaches, vanilla, and cinnamon with a splash of bourbon in the batter and a dollop of fresh cream in the filling!? Oh yes. I was already in a swoon.

RECIPE CONTINUES

1. Preheat the oven to 350°F. Line three 8-by-13-inch cookie sheets with parchment paper.

2. In a large bowl, sift together the flour, baking powder, baking soda, and salt. Whisk the dry ingredients until they're evenly distributed.

3. In another large bowl, cream the sugar and butter with a mixer on medium speed. Add the egg yolks to the creamed ingredients, and mix on medium. Add the egg whites and vanilla, and mix on medium-high until the mixture looks like dense pudding. Then add the reserved peaches, and mix on high.

4. Alternate adding the dry ingredients and the buttermilk to the egg mixture, mixing on medium speed after each addition. Then add the sour cream, and mix well.

5. Using a tablespoon or a pastry bag, drop 1½-inch rounds of batter on the prepared cookie sheets, leaving 1 inch between each round. Bake them approximately 8 minutes, or until the gob domes have risen. Remove the gobs to wire rack to cool.

1. Cream together the butter and cream cheese with a mixer on medium speed.

2. Add the vanilla, crème fraîche, 1 tablespoon of lemon juice, 3 tablespoons of peach-bourbon syrup, and the confectioners' sugar; beat on medium-high. Taste and add another tablespoon of lemon juice or peach-bourbon syrup if you like.

3. To frost the gobs, flip the baked gob domes over on a cookie sheet and match up pairs of similarly shaped domes. Add 1 tablespoon of filling to the flat side of an overturned dome, then place another dome on top, sandwich-style. Allow the gobs to fully set by refrigerating them on a baking sheet for at least 1 hour. Wrap the gobs in plastic wrap to prevent them from drying out.

FOR THE BATTER

- **4 cups plus 2 tablespoons** all-purpose **FLOUR**
- **½ teaspoon BAKING POWDER**
- **1½ teaspoons BAKING SODA**
- **1 teaspoon SALT**
- **2 cups SUGAR**, sifted
- **8 tablespoons UNSALTED BUTTER**, softened, cut in ½-inch cubes
- **2 EGGS**, separated, at room temperature
- **1 teaspoon VANILLA EXTRACT**
- **½ cup PEACHES** reserved from peach-bourbon syrup (recipe follows)
- **1 cup BUTTERMILK**, at room temperature
- **2 tablespoons SOUR CREAM**

FOR THE FILLING

- **8 tablespoons UNSALTED BUTTER**, softened, cut in ½-inch cubes
- **12 tablespoons CREAM CHEESE**, softened, cut in ½-inch cubes
- **1 teaspoon VANILLA EXTRACT**
- **2 teaspoons CRÈME FRAÎCHE**
- **1 to 2 tablespoons fresh LEMON JUICE**
- **3 to 4 tablespoons PEACH-BOURBON SYRUP** (recipe follows)
- **2 cups CONFECTIONERS' SUGAR**, sifted

1. Place the sugar, peaches and their skins, vanilla bean seeds, cinnamon stick, bourbon, and water in a saucepan. Bring the liquid to a boil over medium heat, stirring to dissolve the sugar.

2. Reduce the heat to low and simmer, stirring occasionally, until the mixture reduces by about half (about 20 minutes).

3. Add the lemon juice to the syrup and stir well. Remove the pan from the heat, and set it aside, covered, to let the syrup steep for at least 20 minutes.

4. Remove the peach skins, cinnamon stick, and vanilla bean. Strain the peaches from the syrup, reserving the peaches for the gob batter and the syrup for the gob filling; press the peaches to extract as much liquid as possible. The syrup will keep, tightly covered, in a fridge for up to 2 weeks.

FOR THE

PEACH-BOURBON SYRUP

1 cup SUGAR

Approximately 4 medium-sized PEACHES coarsely chopped, pitted, with skins removed and reserved

1 VANILLA BEAN, split, seeds scraped and reserved

1 CINNAMON STICK

¼ cup BOURBON

½ cup WATER

JUICE of 1 LEMON

CARROT CAKE
GOBS WITH CITRUS CREAM CHEESE FILLING

Carrot cake—for years the words made me shudder. There are a lot of bad carrot cakes out there, and I think I've had them all. Dry, with an uneven distribution of ingredients, they often have little flavor, poor texture, and what I call a "high kack factor": the ability to induce a breath-snatching cough.

So why even bother with a carrot cake gob?

Shopping for ingredients at the Saturday farmer's market often determines what gobs I'll bake for the coming week, and one day my eye was drawn to the beautiful orange of the organic carrots. I picked them up, and they had an aroma as clean and fresh as the late-spring morning.

When I cut into them at home, they were deliciously sweet and bright, not at all like the pithy roots I'd been accustomed to eating. In spite of my carrot cake prejudice, I thought a gob baked with these—along with some organic ginger and organic orange—could taste only of goodness. I was right. This recipe is easy and has been known to convert even the most hard-core of carrot cake haters.

1. Preheat the oven to 350°F. Line three 8-by-13-inch cookie sheets with parchment paper.

2. Place grated carrots, ginger, and orange zest in food processor, and pulse until they're evenly distributed. Set them aside.

3. In a large bowl, sift together the flour, cinnamon, baking powder, baking soda, and salt. Whisk the dry ingredients until they're evenly distributed.

4. In another large bowl, cream the sugar and butter with a mixer on medium speed. Add the egg yolks to the creamed ingredients and mix on medium. Then add the egg whites and vanilla and mix on medium-high until the mixture looks like dense pudding. Add the carrot-ginger-orange mixture and blend on high.

5. Alternate adding the dry ingredients and the buttermilk to the egg mixture, mixing on medium speed after each addition. Then add the sour cream and mix well.

6. Using a tablespoon or a pastry bag, drop 1½-inch rounds of batter on the prepared cookie sheets, leaving 1 inch between each round. Bake them approximately 8 minutes, or until the gob domes have risen. Remove the gobs to a wire rack to cool.

1. Cream together the butter and cream cheese with a mixer on medium speed.

2. Add the vanilla, sour cream, 1 tablespoon of lemon juice, 1 tablespoon of orange juice, and the confectioners' sugar, and beat on medium-high; scrape the bowl with a spatula if necessary to reincorporate the ingredients. Taste and add another tablespoon of lemon juice or orange juice if you like.

3. To frost the gobs, flip the baked gob domes over on a baking sheet and match up pairs of similarly shaped domes. Add 1 tablespoon of filling to the flat side of an overturned dome, then place another dome on top, sandwich-style. Allow the gobs to fully set by refrigerating them on a baking sheet for at least 1 hour. Wrap the gobs in plastic wrap to prevent them from drying out.

FOR THE BATTER

- ½ cup peeled, **GRATED CARROTS** (preferably organic)
- 1 tablespoon grated fresh **GINGER**
- 2 tablespoons **ORANGE ZEST**
- 4 cups all-purpose **FLOUR**
- 1 tablespoon **CINNAMON**
- ½ teaspoon **BAKING POWDER**
- 1½ teaspoons **BAKING SODA**
- 1 teaspoon **SALT**
- 2 cups **SUGAR**, sifted
- 8 tablespoons **UNSALTED BUTTER**, softened, cut in ½-inch cubes
- 2 **EGGS**, separated, at room temperature
- 1 teaspoon **VANILLA EXTRACT**
- 1 cup **BUTTERMILK**, at room temperature
- 2 tablespoons **SOUR CREAM**

FOR THE FILLING

- 4 tablespoons **UNSALTED BUTTER, SOFTENED**, cut in ½-inch cubes
- 16 tablespoons **CREAM CHEESE**, cut in ½-inch cubes
- 1 teaspoon **VANILLA EXTRACT**
- 2 tablespoons **SOUR CREAM**
- 1 to 2 tablespoons fresh **LEMON JUICE**
- 1 to 2 tablespoons fresh **ORANGE JUICE**
- 2 cups **CONFECTIONERS' SUGAR**, sifted

STRAWBERRY-BASIL "SHORTCAKE" GOBS

The Fourth of July weekend was approaching, and I thought I'd gob up the holiday's traditional picnic dessert: strawberry shortcake.

After a few unsuccessful attempts at making a more "shortcake-y" gob, I decided to stick with the batter formula I'd perfected and to put my energy into creating a mind-blowing filling. The strawberries in season had a naturally herbal scent on first whiff, followed by a distinctively sweet aroma. I played up the herbal note with fresh basil, which I added to a strawberry syrup. After straining the syrup, I couldn't leave aside the sweet, reduced strawberries. So I added those to the crème fraîche–laced filling.

1. Preheat the oven to 350°F. Line three 8-by-13-inch cookie sheets with parchment paper.

2. In a large bowl, sift together the flour, baking powder, baking soda, and salt. Whisk the dry ingredients until they're evenly distributed.

3. In another large bowl, cream the sugar and butter with a mixer on medium speed. Add the egg yolks to the creamed ingredients, and mix on medium. Then add the egg whites and vanilla, and mix on medium-high until the mixture looks like dense pudding.

4. Alternate adding the dry ingredients and the buttermilk to the egg mixture, mixing on medium speed after each addition. Then add the sour cream, and mix well.

5. Using a tablespoon or a pastry bag, drop 1½-inch rounds of batter on the prepared cookie sheets, leaving 1 inch between each round. Bake them approximately 8 minutes, or until the gob domes have risen. Remove the gobs to a wire rack to cool.

1. Cream together the butter and cream cheese with a mixer on medium speed.

2. Add the vanilla, crème fraîche, 1 tablespoon of lemon juice, 2 tablespoons of strawberry-basil syrup, and confectioners' sugar, and beat on medium-high; scrape the bowl with a spatula if necessary to reincorporate the ingredients. Taste and add another tablespoon of lemon juice or strawberry-basil syrup if you like.

3. Add the fresh strawberries and the reserved strawberries and blend until they're incorporated.

4. To frost the gobs, flip the baked gob domes over on a baking sheet and match up pairs of similarly shaped domes. Add 1 tablespoon of filling to the flat side of an overturned dome, then place another dome on top, sandwich-style. Allow the gobs to fully set by refrigerating them on a baking sheet for at least 1 hour. Wrap the gobs in plastic wrap to prevent them from drying out.

FOR THE BATTER

- 4 cups plus 2 tablespoons all-purpose FLOUR
- ½ teaspoon BAKING POWDER
- 1½ teaspoons BAKING SODA
- 1 teaspoon SALT
- 2 cups SUGAR, sifted
- 8 tablespoons UNSALTED BUTTER, softened, cut in ½-inch cubes
- 2 EGGS, separated, at room temperature
- 1 tablespoon LEMON ZEST
- 1 teaspoon VANILLA EXTRACT
- 1 cup BUTTERMILK, at room temperature
- 2 tablespoons SOUR CREAM

FOR THE FILLING

- 8 tablespoons UNSALTED BUTTER, softened, cut in ½-inch cubes
- 12 tablespoons CREAM CHEESE, cut in ½-inch cubes
- 1 teaspoon VANILLA EXTRACT
- 1 tablespoon CRÈME FRAÎCHE
- 1 to 2 tablespoons fresh LEMON JUICE
- 2 to 3 tablespoons STRAWBERRY-BASIL SYRUP (recipe follows)
- 2 cups CONFECTIONERS' SUGAR, sifted
- ¼ cup fresh STRAWBERRIES, finely diced
- ¼ cup STRAWBERRIES reserved from strawberry-basil syrup

1. Place the sugar, strawberries, basil, and water in a saucepan. Bring the liquid to a boil over medium heat, stirring to dissolve the sugar.

2. Reduce the heat to low, and simmer, stirring occasionally, until the mixture reduces by about half (about 15 minutes).

3. Add the lemon juice to the syrup and stir well. Remove the pan from the heat and set it aside, covered, to let the syrup steep for at least 20 minutes.

4. Remove the basil leaves. Strain the strawberries from the syrup, reserving the strawberries for the gob batter and the syrup for the gob filling; press the strawberries to extract as much liquid as possible. The syrup will keep, tightly covered, in a fridge for up to 2 weeks.

FOR THE

STRAWBERRY-BASIL SYRUP

- 1 cup **SUGAR**
- 2 cups fresh **STRAWBERRIES**, stems removed and coarsely chopped
- 1 cup loosely packed whole **BASIL LEAVES**, bruised with back of knife
- ½ cup **WATER**
- Juice of 1 **LEMON**

MATCHA GREEN TEA GOBS
WITH Lemongrass-Ginger FILLING

One of my favorite discoveries from my local farmer's market is fresh Vietnamese coriander, or rau ram. I knew that its herbal flavor took well to sweet dishes, so using rau ram in a gob filling was a no-brainer. I decided to match it with a gob cake flavored with green tea.

Baking a green tea gob turned into an education in the use of quality ingredients. The first batch was flavorful when it was freshly made, but within hours it started to take on a metallic taste. Before making my next batch, I went to the store, assessed my green tea options, and decided to take a hit for gob lovers everywhere. I chose one of the more expensive brands of matcha (a powdered tea) and headed back into the kitchen.

When baked with a quality tea (I like DōMatcha brand), the flavor of these gobs is as beguiling as anything I've ever baked. The Matcha Green Tea Gob is one of Gobba Gobba Hey's most requested.

NOTE: Since the rau ram season is short, I've often had to make the filling without it. The result is still good, though maybe not as exotic sounding.

RECIPE CONTINUES

1. Preheat the oven to 350°F. Line three 8-by-13-inch cookie sheets with parchment paper.

2. In a large bowl, sift together the flour, matcha powder, baking powder, baking soda, and salt. Whisk the dry ingredients until they're evenly green in color.

3. In another large bowl, cream the sugar and butter with a mixer on medium speed. Add the egg yolks to the creamed ingredients and mix on medium. Then add the egg whites and vanilla, and mix on medium-high until the mixture looks like dense pudding.

4. Alternate adding the dry ingredients and the buttermilk to the egg mixture, mixing on medium speed after each addition. Then add the sour cream, and mix well.

5. Using a tablespoon or a pastry bag, drop 1½-inch rounds of batter on the prepared cookie sheets, leaving 1 inch between each round. Bake them approximately 8 minutes, or until the gob domes have risen. Remove the gobs to a wire rack to cool.

FOR THE BATTER

- **4 cups all-purpose FLOUR**
- **¼ cup highest-quality MATCHA GREEN TEA POWDER**
- **½ teaspoon BAKING POWDER**
- **1½ teaspoons BAKING SODA**
- **1 teaspoon SALT**
- **2 cups SUGAR, sifted**
- **8 tablespoons UNSALTED BUTTER, softened, cut in ½-inch cubes**
- **2 EGGS, separated, at room temperature**
- **1 teaspoon VANILLA EXTRACT**
- **1 cup BUTTERMILK, at room temperature**
- **2 tablespoons SOUR CREAM**

1. Cream together the butter and cream cheese with a mixer on medium speed.

2. Add the vanilla, 1 teaspoon of lemon juice, 3 tablespoons of lemongrass-ginger syrup, and the confectioners' sugar, and beat on medium-high; scrape the bowl with a spatula if necessary to reincorporate the ingredients. Taste and add another teaspoon of lemon juice or tablespoon of lemongrass-ginger syrup if you like.

3. To the frost the gobs, flip the baked gob domes over on a cookie sheet and match up pairs of similarly shaped domes. Add 1 tablespoon of filling to the flat side of an overturned dome, then place another dome on top, sandwich-style. Allow the gobs to fully set by refrigerating them on a baking sheet for at least 1 hour. Wrap the gobs in plastic wrap to prevent them from drying out.

FOR THE FILLING

- **8 tablespoons UNSALTED BUTTER, softened, cut in ½-inch cubes**
- **12 tablespoons CREAM CHEESE, cut in ½-inch cubes**
- **1 teaspoon VANILLA EXTRACT**
- **1 to 2 teaspoons fresh LEMON JUICE**
- **3 to 4 tablespoons LEMONGRASS-GINGER SYRUP (recipe follows)**
- **2 cups CONFECTIONERS' SUGAR, sifted**

1. Place the sugar, ginger, lemongrass, and water in a saucepan. Bring the liquid to a boil over medium heat, stirring to dissolve the sugar.

2. Add the lemon juice and the rau ram leaves, if using, to the syrup, and stir well. Remove the pan from the heat and set aside, covered, to let the syrup steep for at least 20 minutes.

3. Strain out the rounds of lemongrass, rau ram leaves, and ginger and lemon seeds and pulp, and reserve the syrup for the gob filling. The syrup will keep, tightly covered, in a fridge for up to 1 week if you've added the rau ram, and up to 2 weeks without it.

FOR THE

LEMONGRASS-GINGER SYRUP

1 cup **SUGAR**

2-inch piece fresh **GINGER**, sliced into four or five rounds, skin peeled

½ cup **LEMONGRASS** (about 3 stalks), outer husk and bottom tip removed, sliced in rounds

½ cup **WATER**

Juice of 1 **LEMON**

½ cup loosely packed **RAU RAM LEAVES** (optional)

ORANGE-PISTACHIO GOBS

I had been writing new recipes weekly, allowing instinct and a learn-as-I-go enthusiasm to guide my recipe testing, when I had my first catastrophe in the kitchen.

It probably won't surprise experienced bakers to know that the agent of misfortune was a nut—almost three quarters of a cup of pistachios, to be exact.

My error? Grinding them. I'd originally wanted the pistachios to have a fine, almost flourlike consistency, so after lightly roasting them to intensify their flavor, I dumped them into my food processor and gave the blade a good whirl. The nuts were chopped, but they weren't as powdery as I hoped. I decided the pulse button needed a heavier hand. At first I watched, happily, as the nuts were pulverized into dust. But triumph turned to dismay when, in an instant, the dust regrouped into a hard clump. I'd made pistachio butter.

Still, I wouldn't accept defeat. By beating the nut butter in with the eggs, sugar, and butter before I added the flour, I was able to save the pistachios—and my dream of a deliciously nutty gob.

Orange zest helps keep these gobs moist and complements the pistachios in flavor and aroma.

1. Preheat the oven to 350°F. Line three 8-by-13-inch cookie sheets with parchment paper.

2. Shell the pistachios, then lightly roast them in a frying pan over medium heat, shaking the pan often. When the nuts start to release their aroma, (approximately 3 minutes), remove them from the heat. Set the nuts aside to cool, then place them in a food processor and grind them into a fine powder. If a butter a forms, don't worry; it will still beat into the batter.

3. In a large bowl, sift together the flour, baking powder, baking soda, and salt. Whisk the dry ingredients until they're evenly distributed.

4. In another large bowl, cream the sugar and butter with a mixer on medium speed. Add the egg yolks to the creamed ingredients, and mix on medium. Add the egg whites and vanilla, and mix on medium-high until the mixture looks like dense pudding. Add the ground pistachios and orange zest, and beat on high.

5. Alternate adding the dry ingredients and the buttermilk to the egg mixture, mixing on medium speed after each addition. Then add the sour cream, and mix well.

6. Using a tablespoon or a pastry bag, drop 1½-inch rounds of batter on the prepared cookie sheets, leaving 1 inch between each round. Bake them approximately 8 minutes, or until the gob domes have risen. Remove the gobs to a wire rack to cool.

1. Cream together the butter and cream cheese with a mixer on medium speed.

2. Add the vanilla, 1 tablespoon of lemon juice, 2 tablespoons of orange juice, and the confectioners' sugar, and beat on medium-high; scrape the bowl with a spatula if necessary to reincorporate the ingredients. Taste and add another tablespoon of lemon juice or orange juice if you like.

3. To frost the gobs, flip the baked gob domes over on a cookie sheet and match up pairs of similarly shaped domes. Add 1 tablespoon of filling to the flat side of an overturned dome, then place another dome on top, sandwich-style. Allow the gobs to fully set by refrigerating them on a baking sheet for at least 1 hour. Wrap the gobs in plastic wrap to prevent them from drying out.

FOR THE BATTER

- 1 cup PISTACHIOS in shells
- 4 cups all-purpose FLOUR
- ½ teaspoon BAKING POWDER
- 1½ teaspoons BAKING SODA
- 1 teaspoon SALT
- 2 cups SUGAR, sifted
- 8 tablespoons UNSALTED BUTTER, softened, cut in ½-inch cubes
- 2 EGGS, separated, at room temperature
- 1 teaspoon VANILLA EXTRACT
- 2 tablespoons ORANGE ZEST
- 1 cup BUTTERMILK, at room temperature
- 2 tablespoons SOUR CREAM

FOR THE FILLING

- 8 tablespoons UNSALTED BUTTER, softened, cut in ½-inch cubes
- 12 tablespoons CREAM CHEESE, cut in ½-inch cubes
- 1 teaspoon VANILLA EXTRACT
- 1 to 2 tablespoons fresh LEMON JUICE
- 3 to 4 tablespoons fresh ORANGE JUICE
- 2 cups CONFECTIONERS' SUGAR, sifted

Apricot GOBS
WITH ALMOND FILLING

By the middle of Gobba Gobba Hey's first summer, I'd received an education—both in and out of the kitchen—in the local growing cycles in and near my new hometown. One of the pleasures of shopping at the farmer's market was learning to appreciate the regional growing seasons. When one harvest would end, I'd miss its bounty but also look forward to the organically grown treasures the next harvest would bring.

It was late July when I overheard a farmer's market vendor say, "Yeah, only about two weeks or so left in the apricot season," as she handed over a bag plump with the golden fruit. Only two weeks left? And I hadn't even tried to make an apricot-flavored gob yet!? I needed to get moving.

A familiar presence on my family's holiday dessert trays were Hungarian kifle, a cookie filled with apricot preserves. I thought I would mix things up a little by using the fruit in the gob batter, and complementing the warmth of the apricot flavor with a cool, lemony almond filling. I already knew that apricot and almond flavors enhanced each other, but only later did I learn that the two are actually from the same genus, Prunus, which also includes cherries, plums, and peaches.

My gob-side education continued!

1. Preheat the oven to 350°F. Line three 8-by-13-inch cookie sheets with parchment paper.

2. In a large bowl, sift together the flour, baking powder, baking soda, and salt. Whisk the dry ingredients until they're evenly distributed.

3. In another large bowl, cream the sugar and butter with a mixer on medium speed. Add the egg yolks to the creamed ingredients, and mix on medium. Then add the egg whites and vanilla, and mix on medium-high until the mixture looks like dense pudding. Add the reserved apricots, and mix on high until they're thoroughly blended.

4. Alternate adding the dry ingredients and the buttermilk to the egg mixture, mixing on medium speed after each addition. Then add the sour cream, and mix well.

5. Using a tablespoon or a pastry bag, drop 1½-inch rounds of batter on the prepared cookie sheets, leaving 1 inch between each round. Bake them approximately 8 minutes, or until the gob domes have risen. Remove the gobs to a wire rack to cool.

1. Cream together the butter and cream cheese with a mixer on medium speed.

2. Add the vanilla, crème fraîche, grated almond paste, 1 tablespoon of lemon juice, 3 tablespoons of apricot syrup, and the confectioners' sugar, and beat on medium-high; scrape the bowl with a spatula if necessary to reincorporate the ingredients. Taste and add another tablespoon of lemon juice or apricot syrup if you like.

3. To frost the gobs, flip the baked gob domes over on a cookie sheet and match up pairs of similarly shaped domes. Add 1 tablespoon of filling to the flat side of an overturned dome, then place another dome on top, sandwich-style. Allow the gobs to fully set by refrigerating them on a baking sheet for at least 1 hour. Wrap the gobs in plastic wrap to prevent them from drying out.

FOR THE BATTER

- 4 cups plus 2 tablespoons all-purpose FLOUR
- ½ teaspoon BAKING POWDER
- 1½ teaspoons BAKING SODA
- 1 teaspoon SALT
- 2 cups SUGAR, sifted
- 8 tablespoons UNSALTED BUTTER, softened, cut in ½-inch cubes
- 2 EGGS, at room temperature
- 1 teaspoon VANILLA EXTRACT
- ½ cup APRICOTS reserved from apricot syrup (recipe follows)
- 1 cup BUTTERMILK, at room temperature
- 2 tablespoons SOUR CREAM

FOR THE FILLING

- 8 tablespoons UNSALTED BUTTER, softened, cut in ½-inch cubes
- 8 tablespoons CREAM CHEESE, cut in ½-inch cubes
- 1 teaspoon VANILLA EXTRACT
- 2 tablespoons CRÈME FRAÎCHE
- ½ cup ALMOND PASTE, finely grated
- 1 to 2 tablespoons fresh LEMON JUICE
- 3 to 4 tablespoons APRICOT SYRUP (recipe follows)
- 2 cups CONFECTIONERS' SUGAR, sifted

1. Place the sugar, apricots, and water in a saucepan. Bring the liquid to a boil over medium heat, stirring to dissolve the sugar.

2. Reduce the heat to low and simmer, stirring occasionally, until the mixture reduces by about half (about 15 minutes).

3. Add the lemon juice to the syrup, and stir well. Remove the pan from the heat and set it aside, covered, to let the syrup steep for at least 20 minutes.

4. Strain the mixture, reserving the apricots for the gob batter and the syrup for the gob filling; press the apricots to extract as much liquid as possible. The syrup will keep, tightly covered, in fridge for up to 2 weeks.

FOR THE

APRICOT SYRUP

1 cup SUGAR

2 cups fresh APRICOTS, pitted and coarsely chopped

½ cup WATER

JUICE of 1 LEMON

LEMON GOBS
WITH **BLACKBERRY THYME** FILLING

Blackberries were in high season when I first decided to put them in a gob, paired with the flavors of lemon and thyme. My original idea to use the berries in the batter, though, was a flop. I have since affectionately referred to the confections from that first experiment as the Goth Gobs. Blue-black, and with nubs of berries poking through the side of their dark domes, they looked more like hand-thrown weapons than sugary treats. They were also the unappetizing color of a bruise.

I restructured the recipe, combining the blackberry, lemon, and thyme to make a beautiful syrup for the filling, and relied on lemon zest to flavor the cake.

The flavors complement one another nicely, and the tang of crème fraîche gives the blackberry-flavored filling a mysterious and seductive edge.

RECIPE CONTINUES

1. Preheat the oven to 350°F. Line three 8-by-13-inch cookie sheets with parchment paper.

2. In a large bowl, sift together the flour, baking powder, baking soda, and salt. Whisk the dry ingredients until they're evenly distributed

3. In another large bowl, cream the sugar and butter with a mixer on medium speed. Add the egg yolks to the creamed ingredients, and mix on medium. Then add the egg whites and vanilla, and mix on medium-high until the mixture looks like dense pudding. Add the lemon zest, and mix on high until it's well blended.

4. Alternate adding the dry ingredients and the buttermilk to the egg mixture, mixing on medium speed after each addition. Then add the sour cream, and mix well.

5. Using a tablespoon or a pastry bag, drop 1½-inch rounds of batter on the prepared cookie sheets, leaving 1 inch between each round. Bake them approximately 8 minutes, or until the gob domes have risen. Remove the gobs to a wire rack to cool.

1. Cream together the butter and cream cheese with a mixer on medium speed.

2. Add the vanilla, crème fraîche, 1 teaspoon of lemon juice, 3 tablespoons of blackberry-lemon-thyme syrup, and the confectioners' sugar, and beat on medium-high; scrape the bowl with a spatula to reincorporate the ingredients if necessary. Taste and add another teaspoon of lemon juice or tablespoon of blackberry-lemon-thyme syrup if you like.

3. To frost the gobs, flip the baked gob domes over on a cookie sheet and match up pairs of similarly shaped domes. Add 1 tablespoon of filling to the flat side of an overturned dome, then place another dome on top, sandwich-style. Allow the gobs to fully set by refrigerating them on a baking sheet for at least 1 hour. Cover the gobs with plastic wrap to prevent them from drying out.

FOR THE BATTER

- 4¼ cups all-purpose FLOUR
- ½ teaspoon BAKING POWDER
- 1½ teaspoons BAKING SODA
- 1 teaspoon SALT
- 2 cups SUGAR, sifted
- 8 tablespoons UNSALTED BUTTER, softened, cut in ½-inch cubes
- 2 EGGS, separated, at room temperature
- 1 teaspoon VANILLA EXTRACT
- 2 tablespoons LEMON ZEST
- 1 cup BUTTERMILK, at room temperature
- 2 tablespoons SOUR CREAM

FOR THE FILLING

- 8 tablespoons UNSALTED BUTTER, softened, cut in ½-inch cubes
- 12 tablespoons CREAM CHEESE, cut in ½-inch cubes
- 1 teaspoon VANILLA EXTRACT
- 1 tablespoon CRÈME FRAÎCHE
- 1 to 2 teaspoons fresh LEMON JUICE
- 3 to 4 tablespoons BLACKBERRY-LEMON-THYME SYRUP (recipe follows)
- 2 cups CONFECTIONERS' SUGAR, sifted

1. Place the blackberries, sugar, thyme sprigs, and water in a saucepan. Bring the liquid to a boil over medium heat, stirring to dissolve the sugar.

2. Reduce the heat to low and simmer, stirring occasionally, until the mixture reduces by about half (about 15 minutes).

3. Add the lemon juice to the syrup and stir well. Remove the pan from the heat and set it aside covered, to steep for the syrup for at least 20 minutes.

4. Remove the thyme sprigs and strain the syrup, reserving it for the gob filling; press the blackberries to extract as much liquid as possible. The syrup will keep, tightly covered, in the fridge for up to 2 weeks.

FOR THE

BLACKBERRY-LEMON-THYME SYRUP

2 cups fresh BLACKBERRIES

1 cup SUGAR

5 to 7 fresh THYME SPRIGS

½ cup WATER

JUICE of 2 LEMONS

CHOCOLATE-FENNEL GOBS
WITH Raspberry-Absinthe FILLING

This gob recipe was conceived in one of my more experimental moods, but the original seed of the idea actually came from my parents. When I was young, they used to bake cakes with the bowling-pin-size zucchini that came out of their garden, because the vegetable moistened the batter.

I figured fennel could work the same way in a gob, and I was right. I paired the earthy flavor of fennel with chocolate, and together they worked as the perfect conduit for the bright, adventurous raspberry and absinthe in the filling.

If you don't have access to absinthe, Pernod or even anise extract will do. If you do use the spirit, please proceed cautiously with your taste testing. After baking an early batch that was slathered with absinthe-heavy filling, I came home late one night with a serious craving, opened the fridge where the gobs were stored, and ate five of the absinthe-drenched gobs, one after the other in rapid succession. I never even closed the refrigerator door. When I woke up nine hours later, I had a stupid smile and a smudge of chocolate in the corner of my mouth.

The recipe has since been modified for the safety of all.

1. Preheat the oven to 350°F. Line three 8-by-13-inch cookie sheets with parchment paper.

2. In a large bowl, sift together the flour, cocoa powder, baking powder, baking soda, and salt. Whisk the dry ingredients until they're evenly distributed.

3. In another large bowl, cream the sugar and butter with a mixer on medium speed. Add the egg yolks to the creamed ingredients, and mix on medium. Then add the egg whites and vanilla, and mix on medium-high until the mixture looks like dense pudding. Add the fennel, and mix on high.

4. Alternate adding the dry ingredients and the buttermilk to the egg mixture, mixing on medium speed after each addition. Then add the sour cream, and mix well.

5. Using a tablespoon or pastry bag, drop 1½-inch rounds of batter on the prepared cookie sheets, leaving 1 inch between each round. Bake them approximately 8 minutes, or until the gob domes have risen. Remove the gobs to a wire rack to cool.

1. Cream together the butter and cream cheese with a mixer on medium speed.

2. Add the vanilla, 1 tablespoon of lemon juice, the absinthe, and the confectioners' sugar, and beat on medium-high; scrape the bowl with a spatula to reincorporate the ingredients if necessary. Taste and add another tablespoon of lemon juice if you like—or if you're daring, another tablespoon of absinthe or Pernod. (A tablespoon of anise extract would suffice here.) Then add the fresh raspberries (or raspberry jam).

3. To frost the gobs, flip the baked gob domes over on a cookie sheet and match up pairs of similarly shaped domes. Add 1 tablespoon of filling to the flat side of an overturned dome, then place another dome on top, sandwich-style. Allow the gobs to fully set by refrigerating them on a baking sheet for at least 1 hour. Cover the gobs with plastic wrap to prevent them from drying out.

FOR THE BATTER

- **4 cups all-purpose FLOUR**
- **½ cup COCOA POWDER**
- **½ teaspoon BAKING POWDER**
- **1½ teaspoons BAKING SODA**
- **1 teaspoon SALT**
- **2 cups SUGAR, sifted**
- **8 tablespoons UNSALTED BUTTER, softened, cut in ½-inch**
- **2 EGGS, separated, at room temperature**
- **1 teaspoon VANILLA EXTRACT**
- **¼ cup grated FENNEL BULB**
- **1 cup BUTTERMILK, at room temperature**
- **2 tablespoons SOUR CREAM**

FOR THE FILLING

- **8 tablespoons UNSALTED BUTTER, SOFTENED, cut in ½-inch cubes**
- **12 tablespoons CREAM CHEESE, cut in ½-inch cubes**
- **1 teaspoon VANILLA EXTRACT**
- **1 to 2 tablespoons fresh LEMON JUICE**
- **3 tablespoons ABSINTHE or Pernod, or if using anise extract use 1 tablespoon and increase lemon juice to 3 tablespoons**
- **2 cups CONFECTIONERS' SUGAR, sifted**
- **¼ cup fresh RASPBERRIES (or 3 tablespoons raspberry jam)**

OATMEAL CREAM GOBS

A portion of the credit for the creation of this gob goes to chef and butcher Ryan Farr of 4505 Meats. I was delivering gobs to him for the Ferry Building's Thursday farmer's market one day when he mused, "Remember those oatmeal pies? The ones your mom would bring home from the grocery store?"

Did I ever. I had a near-addictive relationship with them as a kid—as I did with most treats Little Debbie made. The warm flavor of brown sugar, molasses, and cinnamon mixing with the oats . . . the sweet cream filling oozing out, teasingly, from between the two cookies . . .

"Oh, I remember them, all right, like a first date," I answered.

I ran home, excited to tap into some serious nostalgia. After a bit of trial and error, I finally produced this recipe. I prefer using a coarse cut of oats, like those from Bob's Red Mill, which gives these a great texture. If you want your gobs Little Debbie moist, remove them from the oven before all of the sheen has gone out of the molasses-colored batter, about 30 seconds early.

NOTE: These gobs will resemble cookies as they won't rise as high as other gobs.

1. Preheat the oven to 325°F. Line three 8-by-13-inch cookie sheets with parchment paper.

2. In a large bowl, sift together the flour, cinnamon, ginger, baking powder, baking soda, and salt. Whisk the dry ingredients until they're evenly distributed. Then add the oats and whisk thoroughly.

3. In another large bowl, cream the sugar, brown sugar, butter, and molasses with a mixer on medium speed. Add the egg yolks to the creamed ingredients and beat on medium. Add the egg whites and vanilla and mix on medium-high until the mixture looks fluffy.

4. Alternate adding the dry ingredients and the buttermilk to the egg mixture, mixing on medium speed after each addition.

5. Using a tablespoon or pastry bag, drop 1½-inch rounds of batter on the prepared cookie sheets, leaving 2 inches between each round. Bake them approximately 8 minutes, or until the gob domes have risen. Remove the gobs to a wire rack to cool.

FOR THE BATTER

- 2½ cups all-purpose FLOUR
- 1 tablespoon CINNAMON
- 1 teaspoon GROUND GINGER
- ½ teaspoon BAKING POWDER
- 1 teaspoon BAKING SODA
- 1 teaspoon SALT
- 1½ cup quick-cooking, rolled whole grain OATS (such as Bob's Red Mill)
- 1½ cups SUGAR, sifted
- ½ cup LIGHT BROWN SUGAR, tightly packed
- 8 tablespoons UNSALTED BUTTER, softened, cut in ½-inch cubes
- 1 tablespoon MOLASSES
- 2 EGGS, separated, at room temperature
- 1 teaspoon VANILLA EXTRACT
- 1 cup BUTTERMILK, at room temperature

1. Cream together the butter and cream cheese with a mixer on medium speed.

2. Add the vanilla, 1 tablespoon of lemon juice, and the confectioners' sugar, and beat on medium-high; scrape the bowl with a spatula to reincorporate the ingredients if necessary. Taste and add another tablespoon of lemon juice if you like.

3. To frost the gobs, flip the baked gob domes over on a cookie sheet and match up pairs of similarly shaped domes. Add 1 tablespoon of filling to the flat side of an overturned dome, and then place another dome on top, sandwich-style. Allow the gobs to fully set by refrigerating them on a baking sheet for at least 1 hour. Wrap the gobs in plastic wrap to prevent them from drying out.

FOR THE FILLING

- 8 tablespoons UNSALTED BUTTER, softened, cut in ½-inch cubes
- 12 tablespoons CREAM CHEESE, cut in ½-inch cubes
- 1 tablespoon plus 1 teaspoon VANILLA EXTRACT
- 1 to 2 tablespoons fresh LEMON JUICE
- 2 cups CONFECTIONERS' SUGAR, sifted

SPICED PUMPKIN GOBS WITH CREAM CHEESE FILLING

Along with the Original Chocolate and Vanilla Gob, this pumpkin confection with cream cheese filling is the other iconic gob I long to eat, and bake. Where I grew up, pumpkin gobs were a mainstay of autumn entertaining. Stacked together with dark chocolate gobs on a Halloween party treat table, they made for a delicious display.

I wanted my version of this classic to reflect that seasonal switch to warm aromatic spices, when a whiff of cinnamon can help ward off the chill in the air. But I wanted the real star to be the flavor of the pumpkin itself. That's why I use the aptly named sugar pie pumpkin for this recipe. I cannot recommend them strongly enough. These pumpkins are sweet, but not cloyingly so, and they have just the right amount of pith to stand up to being baked in an oven, boiled in a pot, and then mashed in a food processor.

While it might seem unnecessarily labor-intensive to bake the pumpkin in the oven before boiling it, the extra step will reward you with a deeper orange, autumnal color and a more robust flavor.

1. Preheat the oven to 350°F. Line three 8-by-13-inch cookie sheets with parchment paper.

2. In a large bowl, sift together the flour, ginger, nutmeg, baking powder, baking soda, and salt. Whisk the dry ingredients until they're evenly distributed.

3. In another large bowl, cream the sugar and butter, and molasses with a mixer on medium speed. Add the egg yolks to the creamed ingredients and beatw on medium. Then add the egg whites and vanilla, and mix on medium. Add the pumpkin pulp and blend on medium-high until the mixture looks like dense pudding.

4. Alternate adding the dry ingredients and the buttermilk to the egg mixture, mixing on medium speed after each addition. Then add the sour cream, and mix well.

5. Using a tablespoon or pastry bag, drop 1½-inch rounds of batter on the prepared cookie sheets, leaving 1 inch between each round. Bake them approximately 8 minutes, or until the gob domes have risen. Remove the gobs to a wire rack to cool.

1. Cream together the butter and cream cheese with a mixer on medium speed.

2. Add the vanilla, orange juice, 1 tablespoon of lemon juice, 1 tablespoon of pumpkin syrup, and the confectioners' sugar, and beat on medium-high; scrape the bowl with a spatula to reincorporate the ingredients if necessary. Taste and add another tablespoon of lemon juice or pumpkin syrup if you like.

3. To frost the gobs, flip the baked gob domes over on a cookie sheet and match up pairs of similarly shaped domes. Add 1 tablespoon of filling to the flat side of an overturned dome, and then place another dome on top, sandwich-style. Allow the gobs to fully set by refrigerating them on a baking sheet for at least 1 hour. Wrap the gobs in plastic wrap to prevent them from drying out.

FOR THE BATTER

- **4 cups plus 2 tablespoons all-purpose FLOUR**
- **1 teaspoon ground GINGER**
- **½ teaspoon ground NUTMEG**
- **½ teaspoon BAKING POWDER**
- **1½ teaspoon BAKING SODA**
- **1 teaspoon SALT**
- **2 cups SUGAR, sifted**
- **8 tablespoons UNSALTED BUTTER, softened, cut in ½-inch cubes**
- **2 EGGS, separated, at room temperature**
- **1 teaspoon VANILLA EXTRACT**
- **½ cup PUMPKIN PULP (recipe follows)**
- **1 cup BUTTERMILK, at room temperature**
- **2 tablespoons SOUR CREAM**

FOR THE FILLING

- **4 tablespoons UNSALTED BUTTER, softened, cut in ½-inch cubes**
- **16 tablespoons CREAM CHEESE, cut in ½-inch cubes**
- **1 teaspoon VANILLA EXTRACT**
- **1 tablespoon ORANGE JUICE**
- **1 to 2 tablespoons fresh LEMON JUICE**
- **1 to 2 tablespoons PUMPKIN SYRUP (recipe follows)**
- **2 cups CONFECTIONERS' SUGAR, sifted**

1. Preheat the oven to 300°F.

2. Wash the pumpkin, cut it in half, and peel the skin. Scoop out the seeds and pith and chop the pumpkin meat into 1-inch chunks.

3. Place the pumpkin pieces on a greased baking sheet and slow roast them for 20 minutes, or until the flesh is easily pierced with a fork.

4. Place the brown sugar and water in a saucepan over medium heat, and stir until the sugar dissolves. Add the roasted pumpkin, allspice berries, and cinnamon stick, and bring the mixture to a boil.

5. Reduce the heat to low and simmer, stirring occasionally, until the mixture reduces by about half (about 15 minutes). Press the pumpkin pieces with wooden spoon to help them break down.

6. Add the lemon juice to the pan and stir well. Remove the pan from the heat and set it aside, covered, to let the syrup steep for at least 20 minutes.

7. Remove the allspice berries and cinnamon stick. Strain the mixture, reserving the pumpkin pulp for the gob batter (if the pumpkin is too chunky, the pieces can be pureed in a food processor) and the syrup for the gob filling; press the pumpkin to extract as much liquid as possible. The syrup will keep, tightly covered, in a fridge for up to 1 month.

FOR THE

PUMPKIN PULP AND SYRUP

- 1 small **SUGAR PIE PUMPKIN** (approximately 1½ pounds)
- 1 cup **BROWN SUGAR**
- ½ cup **WATER**
- 5 whole **ALLSPICE BERRIES**
- 1 **CINNAMON STICK**
- **JUICE** of 1 **LEMON**

SPICED PUMPKIN Gobs
WITH BUTTERED-RUM FILLING

Who says the kids should have all the fun at Halloween, right? These are the adult version of the Spiced Pumpkin Gobs with Cream Cheese Filling, perfect for an after-work gathering or a weekend tailgater.

I changed the name of these gobs from Pumpkin Spice to Spiced Pumpkin because I thought the former sounded like a Botero-size singer who might have been booted from a certain British girl group. Still, there is something voluptuous about this confection, from the curvaceous little squash that flavors it to the sassy and spirited spices that provide the accents. And let's not forget about the buttered-rum filling in this version!

This batter is the same as for the Spiced Pumpkin Gobs, page 57, but the butter and rum add a different type of richness to the filling. Rum sweetens so many summery, tropical drinks and dishes, but it brings a luscious warmth to fall and winter recipes too. This is definitely one of those fillings with a mouthfeel that will create spoon lust—you may have trouble keeping yourself from dipping a spoon into the mixing bowl.

RECIPE CONTINUES

1. Follow the batter instructions for Spiced Pumpkin Gobs, page 57.

FOR THE **BATTER**

See ingredients, page 57

1. Melt the butter in a saucepan over medium heat until it's golden and bubbly.

2. Add the brown sugar and 2 tablespoons of rum to the melted butter, and whisk until they're combined. Reduce the heat to low, add the heavy cream and salt, and whisk until all the sugar is melted and the cream is integrated. Remove the pan from the heat and allow the mixture to cool.

3. In a medium bowl, cream the cream cheese. Add the vanilla, 1 tablespoon of lemon juice, the cooled rum-butter mixture, and the confectioners' sugar, and mix thoroughly. Taste and add another tablespoon of lemon juice or rum if you like.

4. To frost the gobs, flip the baked gob domes over on a cookie sheet and match up pairs of similarly shaped domes. Add 1 tablespoon of filling to the flat side of an overturned dome, and then place another dome on top, sandwich-style. Allow the gobs to fully set by refrigerating them on a baking sheet for at least 1 hour. Wrap the gobs in cellophane to prevent them from drying out.

FOR THE **FILLING**

- **8 tablespoons UNSALTED BUTTER, softened, cut in ½-inch cubes**
- **2 cups BROWN SUGAR, firmly packed**
- **2 to 3 tablespoons DARK RUM such as Myers's**
- **1 cup HEAVY CREAM**
- **½ teaspoon SALT**
- **16 tablespoons CREAM CHEESE, cut in ½-inch cubes**
- **½ cup CONFECTIONERS' SUGAR, sifted**
- **1 teaspoon VANILLA EXTRACT**
- **1 to 2 tablespoons fresh LEMON JUICE**

1. Preheat the oven to 350°F. Line three 8-by-13-inch cookie sheets with parchment paper.

2. In a large bowl, sift together the flour, cinnamon, baking powder, baking soda, and salt. Whisk the dry ingredients until they're evenly distributed.

3. In another large bowl, cream the sugar and butter with a mixer on medium speed. Add the egg yolks to the creamed ingredients, and mix on medium. Then add the egg whites and vanilla, and mix on medium-high until the mixture looks like dense pudding. Add the apple pulp and mix on medium-high until the mixture is fluffy.

4. Alternate adding the dry ingredients and the buttermilk to the egg mixture, mixing on medium speed after each addition. Then add the sour cream, and mix well.

5. Using a tablespoon or pastry bag, drop 1½-inch rounds of batter on the prepared cookie sheets, leaving 1 inch between each round. Bake them approximately 8 minutes, or until the gob domes have risen. Remove the gobs to a wire rack to cool.

FOR THE BATTER

- **4 cups plus 2 tablespoons all-purpose FLOUR**
- **2 tablespoons ground CINNAMON**
- **½ teaspoon BAKING POWDER**
- **1½ teaspoons BAKING SODA**
- **1 teaspoon SALT**
- **2 cups SUGAR, sifted**
- **8 tablespoons UNSALTED BUTTER, softened, cut in ½-inch cubes**
- **2 EGGS, at room temperature**
- **1 teaspoon VANILLA EXTRACT**
- **½ cup APPLE PULP (recipe follows)**
- **1 cup BUTTERMILK, at room temperature**
- **2 tablespoons SOUR CREAM**

1. Cream together the butter and cream cheese with a mixer on medium speed.

2. Add the vanilla, sour cream, chestnut puree, 1 tablespoon of lemon juice, and the confectioners' sugar, and beat on medium-high; scrape the bowl with a spatula to reincorporate the ingredients if necessary. Taste and add another tablespoon of lemon juice if you like.

3. To frost the gobs, flip the baked gob domes over on a cookie sheet and match up pairs of similarly shaped domes. Add 1 tablespoon of filling to the flat side of an overturned dome, then place another dome on top, sandwich-style. Allow the gobs to fully set by refrigerating them on a baking sheet for at least 1 hour. Wrap the gobs in plastic wrap to prevent them from drying out.

FOR THE FILLING

- **8 tablespoons UNSALTED BUTTER, softened, cut in ½-inch cubes**
- **8 tablespoons CREAM CHEESE, cut in ½-inch cubes**
- **1 tablespoon VANILLA EXTRACT**
- **2 tablespoons SOUR CREAM**
- **½ cup CHESTNUT PUREE (recipe follows)**
- **1 to 2 tablespoons fresh LEMON JUICE**
- **2 cups CONFECTIONERS' SUGAR, sifted**

APPLE Chestnut GOBS

Aside from pumpkin, I can't think of a baked food with a more autumnal aroma than apples. So even though apples are available year-round in the grocery store, it's best to bake these gobs in fall. That's also the season when you can find bags of freshly picked chestnuts.

Early Americans used to choose a variety of apples when making cider, balancing the sweet and juicy fruit from one tree with the crisp, tart fruit from another, resulting in a pour that was unique to their household. I suggest doing the same when selecting apples for this gob. Each apple variety adds something special to the flavor. I am particularly fond of how the tart Granny Smith plays off of the sweet crispness of McIntosh and Yellow Delicious.

I've made the filling with chestnuts grown in Northern California, and I've also used Italian chestnuts. I find the California specimens easiest to work with, and I prefer their mellow flavor. You can sometimes find chestnuts in a jar at the store, but I urge you to give the richly flavored fresh ones a try. If using jarred chestnuts, skip Steps 1 and 2 when making the chestnut puree.

RECIPE CONTINUES

1. Place the apples, sugar, cinnamon stick, nutmeg, and water in a medium saucepan. Bring the liquid to a boil over medium heat, stirring to dissolve the sugar.

2. Reduce the heat to low and simmer, stirring occasionally, until the apples become soft and the volume reduces to about one cup (about 20 to 30 minutes).

3. Turn off heat, remove the cinnamon stick, and stir in the lemon juice.

4. Strain the apple pulp. Transfer the pulp to a food processor and pulse until the mixture has an applesauce consistency. Reserve the apple pulp for the gob batter.

1. Preheat the oven to 300°F. Prepare an 11-by-13-inch greased cookie sheet.

2. Cut an X at one end of each chestnut so the hull can be easily removed. Spread the chestnuts across the baking sheet and bake them for approximately 30 minutes; check them after 15 minutes to see if the shells are beginning to lift where they've been cut. Once the shells have split, and it appears that the nut meat can easily be removed, take them out of the oven and allow them to cool. When they're cool, carefully pull back the shells and dislodge the meat. It should come out easily in one piece.

3. In a medium saucepan, bring the milk and sugar to a near boil, stirring occasionally to dissolve the sugar.

4. Once it's near boiling, add the shelled chestnut meat, vanilla bean, and salt. Reduce the heat to low and simmer until chestnuts begin to soften. When the chestnuts can be easily pierced with a fork, remove the saucepan from the heat, stir in lemon juice, and allow the mixture to cool.

1. Strain the chestnuts from the liquid and place them in a food processor. Pulse the nuts on high until a loose paste is formed, but be careful not to create chestnut butter! Reserve the chestnuts for the gob filling.

FOR THE APPLE PULP

- **4 medium APPLES, any variety, washed, cored, and cut into ½-inch cubes**
- **½ cup SUGAR**
- **1 CINNAMON STICK**
- **¼ teaspoon NUTMEG (preferably freshly ground)**
- **1 cup WATER**
- **JUICE of ½ LEMON (about 2 tablespoons)**

FOR THE

CHESTNUT PUREE

- **1½ pounds fresh CHESTNUTS (choose intact, unblemished chestnuts if possible)**
- **1 cup MILK**
- **½ cup SUGAR**
- **1 whole VANILLA BEAN**
- **Pinch of KOSHER SALT**
- **JUICE of ½ LEMON (approximately 2 tablespoons)**

NOTE: If using jarred chestnuts out of their shells, skip Steps 1 and 2 and add chestnuts to saucepan in Step 4.

CHOCOLATE-ANCHO-CINNAMON
Gobs WITH Almond-Lemon FILLING

I love the combination of chocolate and chili peppers, and when the selection of seasonal fruits starts getting slim at your farmer's market, it can be fun to turn your attention to different ways to work with chocolate. I first offered this gob around the time of San Francisco's observance of Dia de los Muertos (Day of the Dead), when I wanted to bake a gob that had a Mexican flavor to it.

I experimented with using cayenne and chipotle powder, but in the end I liked the ancho pepper best. It has just the right amount of heat without being too fiery. Ground cinnamon stands up to the ancho's power, and the almond-lemon filling helps tame the flame, for the perfect balance of heat, sweetness, spice, and citrus tang.

Feel free to add more cinnamon if you like, or to set your micrograter over the bowl of batter for a few quick strokes of whole nutmeg zest. For the filling, make sure to use almond paste, not marzipan. Refrigerating the paste for several hours beforehand will make it easy to grate.

1. Preheat the oven to 350°F. Line three 8-by-13-inch cookie sheets with parchment paper.

2. In a large bowl, sift together the flour, cocoa powder, ancho chili powder, cinnamon, baking powder, baking soda, and salt. Whisk the dry ingredients until they're evenly distributed.

3. In another large bowl, cream the sugar and butter with a mixer on medium speed. Add the egg yolks to the creamed ingredients, and mix on medium. Then add the egg whites and vanilla, and mix on medium-high until the mixture looks like dense pudding.

4. Alternate adding the dry ingredients and the buttermilk to the egg mixture, mixing on medium speed after each addition. Then add the sour cream, and mix well.

5. Using a tablespoon or pastry bag, drop 1½-inch rounds of batter on the prepared cookie sheets, leaving 1 inch between each round. Bake them approximately 8 minutes, or until the gob domes have risen. Remove the gobs to a wire rack to cool.

FOR THE BATTER

- 4 cups all-purpose FLOUR
- ½ cup COCOA POWDER
- 2 tablespoons ANCHO CHILI POWDER
- 1½ tablespoons CINNAMON
- ½ teaspoon BAKING POWDER
- 1½ teaspoons BAKING SODA
- 1 teaspoon SALT
- 2 cups SUGAR, sifted
- 8 tablespoons UNSALTED BUTTER, softened, cut in ½-inch cubes
- 2 EGGS, separated, at room temperature
- 1 teaspoon VANILLA EXTRACT
- 1 cup BUTTERMILK, at room temperature
- 2 to 3 tablespoons SOUR CREAM

1. Cream together the butter and cream cheese with a mixer on medium.

2. Add the grated almond paste, vanilla, sour cream, 1 tablespoon of lemon juice, and confectioners' sugar, and beat on medium-high; scrape the bowl with a spatula to reincorporate the ingredients if necessary. Taste and add another tablespoon of lemon juice if you like.

3. To frost the gobs, flip the baked gob domes over on a cookie sheet and match up pairs of similarly shaped domes. Add 1 tablespoon of filling to the flat side of an overturned dome, then place another dome on top, sandwich-style. Allow the gobs to fully set by refrigerating them on a baking sheet for at least 1 hour. Wrap the gobs in plastic wrap to prevent them from drying out.

FOR THE FILLING

- 8 tablespoons UNSALTED BUTTER, SOFTENED, cut in ½-inch cubes
- 8 tablespoons CREAM CHEESE, cut in ½-inch cubes
- ½ cup grated ALMOND PASTE
- 1 teaspoon VANILLA EXTRACT
- 2 tablespoons SOUR CREAM
- 1 to 2 tablespoons fresh LEMON JUICE
- 2 cups CONFECTIONERS' SUGAR, sifted

IRISH COFFEE
GOBS WITH Bushmills & Baileys Irish Cream FILLING

This recipe came about when I was asked to come up with a signature coffee-flavored gob for a new coffeehouse in San Francisco. In my first attempt, I used brewed coffee in the batter, but dark hypno-swirls of java could be seen on top of the baked gobs. Also, it didn't provide the welcoming roasted flavor I wanted. I found the solution in the form of espresso powder.

The pairing of the seductively sweet Baileys Irish Cream with the bite of Bushmills Irish Whiskey in the filling definitely makes this an adult indulgence. I've baked these for several parties, and they're always a hit, especially on St. Patrick's Day. I like to think of this gob as coffee, dessert, and an after-dinner drink—all in one delicious confection!

1. Preheat the oven to 350°F. Line three 8-by-13-inch cookie sheets with parchment paper.

2. In a large bowl, sift together the flour, cocoa powder, espresso powder, baking powder, baking soda, and salt. Whisk the dry ingredients until they're evenly distributed.

3. In another large bowl, cream the sugar and butter with a mixer on medium speed. Add the egg yolks to the creamed ingredients, and mix on medium. Then add the egg whites and vanilla, and mix on medium-high until the mixture looks like dense pudding.

4. Alternate adding the dry ingredients and the buttermilk to the egg mixture, mixing on medium speed after each addition. Then add the sour cream, and mix well.

5. Using a tablespoon or pastry bag, drop 1½-inch rounds of batter on the prepared cookie sheets, leaving 1 inch between each round. Bake them approximately 8 minutes, or until the gob domes have risen. Remove the gobs to a wire rack to cool.

1. Cream together the butter and cream cheese with a mixer on medium speed.

2. Add the vanilla, 1 teaspoon of lemon juice, 2 tablespoons of Baileys, 2 tablespoons of Bushmills, and the confectioners' sugar, and beat on medium-high; scrape the bowl with a spatula to reincorporate the ingredients if necessary. Taste and add another teaspoon of lemon juice or tablespoon of Baileys or Bushmills if you like.

3. To frost the gobs, flip the baked gob domes over on a cookie sheet and match up pairs of similarly shaped domes. Add 1 tablespoon of filling to the flat side of an overturned dome, and then place another dome on top, sandwich-style. Allow the completed the gobs to fully set by refrigerating them on a baking sheet for at least 1 hour. Wrap the gobs in plastic wrap to prevent them from drying out.

FOR THE BATTER

- 4 cups all-purpose **FLOUR**
- ¼ cup plus 2 tablespoons **COCOA POWDER**
- 2 tablespoons **ESPRESSO POWDER**, such as King Arthur
- ½ teaspoon **BAKING POWDER**
- 1½ teaspoons **BAKING SODA**
- 1 teaspoon **SALT**
- 2 cups **SUGAR**, sifted
- 8 tablespoons **UNSALTED BUTTER**, softened, cut in ½-inch cubes
- 2 **EGGS**, separated, at room temperature
- 1 teaspoon **VANILLA**
- 1 cup **BUTTERMILK**, at room temperature
- 2 to 3 tablespoons **SOUR CREAM**

FOR THE FILLING

- 8 tablespoons **UNSALTED BUTTER**, softened, cut in ½-inch cubes
- 12 tablespoons **CREAM CHEESE**, cut in ½-inch cubes
- 1 teaspoon **VANILLA EXTRACT**
- 1 to 2 teaspoons fresh **LEMON JUICE**
- 2 to 3 tablespoons **BAILEYS IRISH CREAM**
- 1 to 2 tablespoons **BUSHMILLS IRISH WHISKEY**
- 2 cups **CONFECTIONERS' SUGAR**, sifted

CHOCOLATE, MOCHA, ALMOND
Gobs WITH SHAVED ALMONDS

Need proof that people love the blend of chocolate, coffee, and almonds? Go into any coffee shop and look at the specialty-drink menu. This recipe is relatively easy and assures that you'll get the most oomph out of each of the three key ingredients. If you want to heighten the nuttiness, you can add an extra half teaspoon of almond extract to the batter. Be judicious, though; the almond paste is more than capable of delivering the goods.

To give the gobs a little textural dimension, sprinkle the inside of each frosted dome with shaved almonds before nestling its other half in place. The shaved almonds provide an unexpected crunch.

Alternatively, you can frost and set the gobs as usual, then roll them like wheels through ground almonds spread on waxed paper.

1. Preheat the oven to 350°F. Line three 8-by-13-inch cookie sheets with parchment paper.

2. In a large bowl, sift together the flour, cocoa powder, espresso powder, baking powder, baking soda, and salt. Whisk the dry ingredients until they're evenly distributed.

3. In another large bowl, cream the sugar and butter with a mixer on medium speed. Add the egg yolks to the creamed ingredients, and mix on medium. Then add the egg whites, vanilla, and almond extract, and mix on medium-high until the mixture looks like dense pudding.

4. Alternate adding the dry ingredients and the buttermilk to the egg mixture, mixing on medium speed after each addition. Then add the sour cream, and mix well.

5. Using a tablespoon or pastry bag, drop 1½-inch rounds of batter on the prepared cookie sheets, leaving 1 inch between each round. Bake them approximately 8 minutes, or until the gob domes have risen. Remove the gobs to a wire rack to cool.

FOR THE BATTER

- 4 cups all-purpose **FLOUR**
- ½ cup **COCOA POWDER**
- 2 tablespoons **ESPRESSO POWDER**, such as King Arthur
- ½ teaspoon **BAKING POWDER**
- 1½ teaspoons **BAKING SODA**
- 1 teaspoon **SALT**
- 2 cups **SUGAR**, sifted
- 8 tablespoons **UNSALTED BUTTER**, softened, cut in ½-inch cubes
- 2 **EGGS**, separated, at room temperature
- ½ teaspoon **VANILLA EXTRACT**
- ½ teaspoon **ALMOND EXTRACT**
- 1 cup **BUTTERMILK**, at room temperature
- 2 tablespoons **SOUR CREAM**

1. Cream the butter and cream cheese together with a mixer on medium. Add grated almond paste. Mix on medium high til thoroughly incorporated

2. Add the vanilla, almond extract, 2 tablespoons of lemon juice, and the confectioners' sugar, and beat on medium-high; scrape the bowl with a spatula to reincorporate the ingredients if necessary. Taste and add another tablespoon of lemon juice if you like.

3. To frost the gobs, flip the baked gob domes over on a cookie sheet and match up pairs of similarly shaped domes. Add 1 tablespoon of filling to the flat side of an overturned dome, and then place another dome on top, sandwich-style. Allow completed the gobs to fully set by refrigerating them on a baking sheet for at least 1 hour. Wrap the gobs in plastic wrap to prevent them from drying out.

FOR THE FILLING

- 8 tablespoons **UNSALTED BUTTER**, softened, cut in ½-inch cubes
- 8 tablespoons **CREAM CHEESE**, cut in ½-inch cubes
- 1 teaspoon **VANILLA EXTRACT**
- 1 teaspoon **ALMOND EXTRACT**
- ½ cup grated **ALMOND PASTE**
- 3 tablespoons fresh **LEMON JUICE**
- 2 cups **CONFECTIONERS' SUGAR**, sifted

CHOCOLATE, ALMOND, COCONUT GOBS

Almond Joy was one of my favorite chocolate bars when I was growing up, and the almond and the toasted-coconut flavor combination—re-created in this gob—remains one of my favorites to this day.

If you want a more traditional chocolate-bar flavor, you can use a cocoa like Hershey's, but I prefer Green & Black's Organic Cocoa in all of my chocolate-flavored gobs. Its complex flavor seems to bring out the subtleties in other ingredients, and coconut and almond are no exception.

The simple filling recipe relies on almond extract for flavoring. Be sure to use a good-quality brand; cheaper almond extracts can have an unpleasant chemical aftertaste. To make this more of an adult confection, you can replace one or even both tablespoons of the almond extract with an almond liqueur such as Disaronno.

1. Follow the batter instructions for S.F. Chocolate Vanilla Gob, page 23.

FOR THE **BATTER**

See ingredients, page 23

1. Cream together the butter and cream cheese with a mixer on medium speed.

2. Add 2 tablespoons of almond extract (or almond liqueur), 1 tablespoon of lemon juice, and the confectioners' sugar, and beat on medium-high; scrape the bowl with a spatula to reincorporate the ingredients if necessary. Taste and add another tablespoon of lemon juice or almond extract (or almond liqueur) if you like.

3. To frost the gobs, flip the baked gob domes over on a cookie sheet and match up pairs of similarly shaped domes. Add 1 tablespoon of filling to the flat side of an overturned dome. When half of the domes are topped with filling, sprinkle coconut shreds and almond slivers atop the filling. Place another dome on top, sandwich-style. Allow the gobs to fully set by refrigerating them on a baking sheet for at least 1 hour. Wrap the gobs in plastic wrap to prevent them from drying out.

FOR THE **FILLING**

- 8 tablespoons **UNSALTED BUTTER**, softened, cut in ½-inch cubes
- 12 tablespoons **CREAM CHEESE**, cut in ½-inch cubes
- 2 to 3 tablespoons **ALMOND EXTRACT (or almond liqueur)**
- 1 to 2 tablespoons fresh **LEMON JUICE**
- 2 cups **CONFECTIONERS' SUGAR**, sifted
- 1 cup **COCONUT**, toasted, for dusting
- ½ cup **SLIVERED ALMOND**, for dusting

GINGERSNAP RASPBERRY GOBS

Gingersnaps are one of my go-to comfort foods, and the Gingersnap Raspberry Gob captures their reassuring and familiar flavor.

This gob has that same "dunk-in-a-glass-of-milk" flavor as the cookie. The first time I baked these, I was so taken in by their aroma that I ate four domes before I even filled them! The brown sugar is a perfect complement to the ground ginger, and the raspberry filling—with both fresh berries and a dollop of jam—sweetens things up.

For a real wow factor, sprinkle the tops of the baked gobs with crystalized ginger shortly after you remove them from the oven. A scant half cup, pulverized in a food processor, is all that is needed to give these already tasty gobs an extra enticing and perky texture.

1. Preheat the oven to 350°F. Line three 8-by-13-inch cookie sheets with parchment paper.

2. In a large bowl, sift together the flour, ginger, cinnamon, baking powder, baking soda, and salt. Whisk the dry ingredients until they're evenly distributed

3. In another large bowl, cream the sugar, brown sugar, and butter with a mixer on medium speed. Add the egg yolks to the creamed ingredients, and mix on medium. Then add the egg whites and vanilla, and mix on medium-high until the mixture looks like dense pudding.

4. Alternate adding the dry ingredients and the buttermilk to the egg mixture, mixing on medium speed after each addition. Then add the sour cream, and mix well.

5. Using a tablespoon or pastry bag, drop 1½-inch rounds of batter on the prepared cookie sheets, leaving 1 inch between each round. Bake them approximately 8 minutes, or until the gob domes have risen. Remove the gobs to a wire rack to cool.

6. If using the crystallized ginger, pulverize in a food processor while the gobs are baking, and sprinkle it over top of the gobs shortly after you remove them from the oven.

1. Cream together the butter and cream cheese with mixer on medium speed.

2. Add the vanilla, sour cream, 1 tablespoon of lemon juice, and the confectioners' sugar, and beat on medium-high; scrape the side of the bowl to reincorporate the ingredients if necessary. Spoon in the raspberry jam or preserves, and mix on high. Add the fresh raspberries, and mix just until they're incorporated. Taste and add another tablespoon of lemon juice if you like.

3. To frost the gobs, flip the baked gob domes over on a cookie sheet and match up pairs of similarly shaped domes. Add 1 tablespoon of filling to the flat side of an overturned dome, then place another dome on top, sandwich-style. Allow the gobs to fully set by refrigerating them for at least 1 hour. Wrap the gobs in plastic wrap to prevent them from drying out.

FOR THE BATTER

- 4 cups plus 2 tablespoons all-purpose FLOUR
- 3 tablespoons ground GINGER
- 1 teaspoon CINNAMON
- ½ teaspoon BAKING POWDER
- 1½ teaspoons BAKING SODA
- 1 teaspoon SALT
- 1½ cups SUGAR, sifted
- ½ cup LIGHT BROWN SUGAR, firmly packed
- 8 tablespoons UNSALTED BUTTER, softened, cut in ½-inch cubes
- 2 EGGS, separated, at room temperature
- 1 teaspoon VANILLA EXTRACT
- 1 cup BUTTERMILK, at room temperature
- 2 tablespoons SOUR CREAM

FOR THE FILLING

- 8 tablespoons UNSALTED BUTTER, softened, cut in ½-inch cubes
- 12 tablespoons CREAM CHEESE, cut in ½-inch cubes
- 1 teaspoon VANILLA EXTRACT
- 2 tablespoons SOUR CREAM
- 1 to 2 tablespoons fresh LEMON JUICE
- 2 cups CONFECTIONERS' SUGAR, sifted
- 2 tablespoons RASPBERRY JAM or raspberry preserves
- ¼ cup fresh RASPBERRIES

NEAPOLITAN GOBS

As a kid, I thought Neapolitan ice cream was the best of all possible worlds: three types of ice cream, evenly distributed in one box. If you dragged a spoon across the top just so, you could get an equal amount of each. Heaven.

Not surprisingly, chocolate, strawberry, and vanilla also make for a tantalizing gob. The trickiest part of making this gob is getting the different-flavored domes to match—sometimes one batch will rise higher than the others, and the assembled gobs can end up lopsided. It helps to use a kitchen scale when measuring the dry ingredients. This will assure that your gobs are similarly and evenly shaped. Make sure the amount of cocoa in the chocolate halves matches the amount of additional flour in the vanilla halves *by weight*.

1. Preheat the oven to 350°F. Line three 8-by-13-inch cookie sheets with parchment paper.

2. In a large bowl, sift together the flour, baking powder, baking soda, and salt. Whisk the dry ingredients until they're evenly distributed.

3. In another large bowl, cream the sugar, butter, and vanilla seeds with a mixer on medium speed. Add the egg yolk to the creamed ingredients, and blend on medium. Then add the egg white and vanilla, and mix on medium-high until the mixture looks like dense pudding.

4. Alternate adding the dry ingredients and the buttermilk to the egg mixture, mixing on medium speed after each addition. Then add the sour cream, and mix well.

5. Using a tablespoon or pastry bag, drop 1½-inch rounds of batter on the prepared cookie sheets, leaving 1 inch between each round. Bake them approximately 8 minutes, or until the gob domes have risen. Remove the gobs to a wire rack to cool.

1. Follow the batter instructions for S.F. Chocolate Vanilla Gob recipe on page 23, but halve all ingredient measurements.

1. Follow the filling and syrup instructions for the Strawberry-Basil "Shortcake" Gobs, page 39–40, but make sure to omit the basil!

2. To frost the gobs, match up pairs of similarly sized vanilla and chocolate gob domes. Using a tablespoon or pastry bag, put 1 tablespoon of the strawberry filling on the flat, bottom half of each pair. Then place the other dome on top, sandwich-style. Allow the gobs to fully set by refrigerating them on a baking sheet for at least 1 hour. Wrap the gobs in plastic wrap to prevent them from drying out.

FOR THE

VANILLA BATTER

- 2¼ cups all-purpose **FLOUR**
- ¼ teaspoon **BAKING POWDER**
- ¾ teaspoon **BAKING SODA**
- ½ teaspoon **SALT**
- 1 cup **SUGAR**, sifted
- 4 tablespoons **UNSALTED BUTTER**, softened, cut in ½-inch cubes
- 1 **VANILLA BEAN**, seeds scraped and ½ reserved (save other half for filling)
- 1 **EGG**, separated, at room temperature
- ½ teaspoon **VANILLA EXTRACT**
- ½ cup **BUTTERMILK**, at room temperature
- 1½ teaspoons sour cream

FOR THE

CHOCOLATE BATTER

See ingredients, page 23

FOR THE **FILLING**

See ingredients, page 39–40

ROOT BEER FLOAT GOBS

Growing up in an area where people brewed their own root beer (among other things) in their basements and backyards, I was determined that any root beer gob I made would start with a root beer flavor made from scratch. I shopped online and in brew shops for sarsaparilla, sassafras, and the other necessary tinctures and extracts.

My first attempt at making a root beer syrup definitely tasted like a "root"—pithy, astringent, and even a little peaty. After I made some adjustments, my next batch was closer to the flavor I was striving for, but it was still too strong. A root beer float should tickle the nose, not drain the sinuses.

I did more research online, visiting blogs by root beer aficionados and bakers alike. According to many of these bloggers, their success was due to one particular ingredient. So I went back to the brew shop, picked up what the experts had recommended, and got down to work. Sure enough, the resulting gobs were delicious, with just the right amount of "fizzy" flavor. The secret to success? Premade root beer extract. You can find it in well-stocked grocery stores, shops that cater to home brewers, or online. The extract is easy to use, the flavor is exactly what you hope it will be, and I can honestly say that when paired with vanilla filling, this gob is a total success.

1. Preheat the oven to 350°F. Line three 8-by-13-inch cookie sheets with parchment paper.

2. In a large bowl, sift together the flour, baking powder, baking soda, and salt. Whisk the dry ingredients until they're evenly distributed.

3. In another large bowl, cream the sugar and butter with a mixer on medium speed. Add the egg yolks to the creamed ingredients, and mix on medium. Then add the egg whites and vanilla, and mix on medium-high until the mixture looks like dense pudding.

4. Alternate adding the dry ingredients and the buttermilk to the egg mixture, mixing on medium speed after each addition. Then add the sour cream, and mix well. Add the root beer extract and mix on high. Add more sour cream, 1 tablespoon at a time, if the batter is too thick.

5. Using a tablespoon or pastry bag, drop 1½-inch rounds of batter on the prepared cookie sheets, leaving 1 inch between each round. Bake them approximately 8 minutes, or until the gob domes have risen. Remove the gobs to a wire rack to cool.

1. Cream together the butter and cream cheese with a mixer on medium speed.

2. Add the vanilla extract, vanilla bean seeds, sour cream, 1 tablespoon of lemon juice, and the confectioners' sugar, and beat on medium-high; scrape the bowl with a spatula to reincorporate the ingredients if necessary. Taste and add another tablespoon of lemon juice if you like.

3. To frost the gobs, flip the baked gob domes over on a cookie sheet and match up pairs of similarly shaped domes. Add 1 tablespoon of filling to the flat side of an overturned dome, then place another dome on top, sandwich-style. Allow the gobs to fully set by refrigerating them on a baking sheet for at least 1 hour. Wrap the gobs in plastic wrap to prevent them from drying out.

FOR THE BATTER

- 4½ cups all-purpose **FLOUR**
- ½ teaspoon **BAKING POWDER**
- 1½ teaspoons **BAKING SODA**
- 1 teaspoon **SALT**
- 2 cups **SUGAR**, sifted
- 8 tablespoons **UNSALTED BUTTER**, softened, cut in ½-inch cubes
- 2 **EGGS**, separated, at room temperature
- 1 teaspoon **VANILLA EXTRACT**
- 1 cup **BUTTERMILK**, at room temperature
- 2 tablespoons **SOUR CREAM**
- 3 tablespoons **ROOT BEER EXTRACT**

FOR THE FILLING

- 8 tablespoons **UNSALTED BUTTER**, softened, cut in ½-inch cubes
- 12 tablespoons **CREAM CHEESE**, cut in ½-inch cubes
- 2 tablespoons **VANILLA EXTRACT**
- 1 large **VANILLA BEAN**, seeds scraped and reserved
- 2 tablespoons **SOUR CREAM**
- 1 to 2 tablespoons fresh **LEMON JUICE**
- 2 cups **CONFECTIONERS' SUGAR**, sifted

VANILLA GOBS
WITH Strawberry-Balsamic FILLING

This was one of the flavors I'd been hoping to experiment with, but I didn't want to make an entire batch, as my pantry wasn't always as full as I'd like. Well, I had procured a sizable stash of organic vanilla beans and had baked an extra batch of vanilla gobs one day. I had also had some leftover strawberry filling in the fridge. Now, I'd been devouring strawberry-balsamic glazes and sauces, slathered on pound cake and oozed over mounds of vanilla ice cream, in restaurants and cafés in and around San Francisco, but I'd never attempted to make my own version. I thought a strawberry filling with a balsamic edge would be just as good between two sexy, sweet vanilla gob domes. I was right.

1. 1. Preheat the oven to 350°F. Line three 8-by-13-inch cookie sheets with parchment paper.

2. In a large bowl, sift together the flour, baking powder, baking soda, and salt. Whisk the dry ingredients until they're evenly distributed.

3. In another large bowl, cream the sugar, butter, and vanilla seeds with a mixer on medium speed. Add the egg yolks to the creamed ingredients, and mix on medium. Add the egg whites, lemon zest, and vanilla extract, and mix on medium-high until the mixture looks like dense pudding.

4. Alternate adding the dry ingredients and the buttermilk to the egg mixture, mixing on medium speed after each addition. Then add the sour cream, and mix well.

5. Using a tablespoon or pastry bag, drop 1½-inch rounds of batter on the prepared cookie sheets, leaving 1 inch between each round. Bake them approximately 8 minutes, or until the gob domes have risen. Remove the gobs to a wire rack to cool.

FOR THE BATTER

- 4½ cups all-purpose FLOUR
- ½ teaspoon BAKING POWDER
- 1½ teaspoons BAKING SODA
- 1 teaspoon SALT
- 2 cups SUGAR, sifted
- 8 tablespoons UNSALTED BUTTER, softened, cut in ½-inch cubes
- 1 large VANILLA BEAN, seeds scraped and reserved
- 2 EGGS, separated, at room temperature
- 2 tablespoons freshly grated LEMON ZEST
- 1 teaspoon VANILLA EXTRACT
- 1 cup BUTTERMILK, at room temperature
- 2 tablespoons SOUR CREAM

1. Cream together the butter and cream cheese with a mixer on medium speed.

2. Add the vanilla, 1 tablespoon of lemon juice, 3 tablespoons of strawberry-balsamic syrup, and the confectioners' sugar, and beat on medium-high; scrape the bowl with a spatula to reincorporate the ingredients if necessary. Taste and add another tablespoon of lemon juice or strawberry-balsamic syrup if you like.

3. To frost the gobs, flip the baked gob domes over on a cookie sheet and match up pairs of similarly shaped domes. Add 1 tablespoon of filling to the flat side of an overturned dome, then place another dome on top, sandwich-style. Allow the gobs to fully set by refrigerating them on a baking sheet for at least 1 hour. Wrap the gobs in plastic wrap to prevent them from drying out.

FOR THE FILLING

- 8 tablespoons UNSALTED BUTTER, softened, cut in ½-inch cubes
- 12 tablespoons CREAM CHEESE, softened, cut in ½-inch cubes
- 1 teaspoon VANILLA EXTRACT
- 1 to 2 tablespoons fresh LEMON JUICE
- 3 to 4 tablespoons STRAWBERRY-BALSAMIC SYRUP (recipe follows)
- 2 cups CONFECTIONERS' SUGAR, sifted

1. Place the strawberries, sugar, and water in a saucepan. Bring the liquid to a boil over medium heat, stirring to dissolve the sugar.

2. Reduce the heat to low and simmer, stirring occasionally, until the mixture reduces by about half (about 15 minutes). Add the balsamic vinegar and lemon juice to the syrup, and stir well. Simmer the mixture for another 5 minutes.

3. Remove the pan from the heat and set it aside, covered, to let the syrup steep for at least 10 minutes.

4. Strain the mixture, reserving the syrup for the gob filling; press the strawberries to extract as much liquid as possible. The syrup will keep, tightly covered, in a fridge for up to 2 weeks. You can use the strawberries on ice cream or tossed in a salad. You can even whip them into the gob filling, but be careful to not overliquefy it and also be mindful of sugar clumps.

FOR THE

STRAWBERRY-BALSAMIC SYRUP

- **2 cups fresh STRAWBERRIES, stems removed, coarsely chopped**
- **1 cup SUGAR**
- **½ cup WATER**
- **1 tablespoon BALSAMIC VINEGAR**
- **1 teaspoon LEMON JUICE**

LEMON POPPY SEED Gobs WITH Blueberry FILLING

I have always associated poppy seeds with Christmas. Bobalky (pronounced *bull-BUY-kee)* are one of the traditional holiday foods from the Hungarian side of my family. These honey-drenched rounds of dough are rolled in poppy seeds and served every year at Christmas Eve dinner. Given my strong seasonal and filial memories of poppy seeds, not to mention my love of citrus flavors in the colder months, it's probably no surprise that Lemon Poppy Seed Gobs are one of my sentimental favorites.

The sunny citrus of the lemon and the slightly nutty flavor of the seeds in these gobs help warm up a morning coffee break in the colder months. Add blueberry filling and you get a downright cheery confection.

RECIPE CONTINUES

1. Preheat the oven to 350°F. Line three 8-by-13-inch cookie sheets with parchment paper.

2. In a large bowl, sift together the flour, baking powder, baking soda, and salt. Whisk the dry ingredients until they're evenly distributed. Add poppy seeds and whisk again.

3. In another large bowl, cream the sugar and butter with a mixer on medium speed. Add the egg yolks to the creamed ingredients, and mix on medium. Then add the egg whites, vanilla, and lemon zest, and mix on medium-high until the mixture looks like dense pudding

4. Alternate adding the dry ingredients and the buttermilk to the egg mixture, mixing on medium speed after each addition. Then add the sour cream, and mix well.

5. Using a tablespoon or pastry bag, drop 1½-inch rounds of batter on the prepared cookie sheets, leaving 1 inch between each round. Bake them approximately 8 minutes, or until the gob domes have risen. Remove the gobs to a wire rack to cool.

FOR THE **BATTER**

- **4 cups plus 2 tablespoons all-purpose FLOUR**
- **½ teaspoon BAKING POWDER**
- **1 teaspoon BAKING SODA**
- **1 teaspoon SALT**
- **2 tablespoons POPPY SEEDS**
- **2 cups SUGAR, sifted**
- **8 tablespoons UNSALTED BUTTER, softened, cut in ½-inch cubes**
- **2 EGGS, separated, at room temperature**
- **1 teaspoon VANILLA EXTRACT**
- **1½ tablespoons LEMON ZEST**
- **1 cup BUTTERMILK, at room temperature**
- **2 tablespoons SOUR CREAM**

1. Cream together the butter and cream cheese with a mixer on medium speed.

2. Add the vanilla, 1 tablespoon of lemon juice, 3 tablespoons of blueberry syrup, and the confectioners' sugar, and mix on medium. Add the reserved blueberries, and beat until the mixture is fluffy; scrape the bowl with a spatula to reincorporate the ingredients if necessary. Taste and add another tablespoon of lemon juice or blueberry syrup if you like.

3. To frost the gobs, flip the baked gob domes over on a cookie sheet and match up pairs of similarly shaped domes. Add 1 tablespoon of filling to the flat side of an overturned dome, then place another dome on top, sandwich-style. Allow the gobs to fully set by refrigerating them on a baking sheet for at least 1 hour. Wrap the gobs in plastic wrap to prevent them from drying out.

FOR THE **FILLING**

- **8 tablespoons UNSALTED BUTTER, softened, cut in ½-inch cubes**
- **12 tablespoons CREAM CHEESE, cut in ½-inch cubes**
- **1 teaspoon VANILLA EXTRACT**
- **1 to 2 tablespoons fresh LEMON JUICE**
- **3 to 4 tablespoons BLUEBERRY SYRUP (recipe follows)**
- **2 cups CONFECTIONERS' SUGAR, sifted**
- **¼ cup BLUEBERRIES reserved from blueberry syrup**

1. Place the blueberries, sugar, water, and lemon juice in a saucepan. Bring the liquid to a near boil, then reduce the heat to low and simmer, stirring occasionally, until the mixture is reduced by half (about 15 minutes).

2. Remove the pan from heat and let the mixture cool.

3. Strain the mixture, reserving the blueberries and the syrup in separate containers for the gob filling.

FOR THE
BLUEBERRY SYRUP

1 cup **BLUEBERRIES**, rinsed well in cold water
½ cup **SUGAR**
½ cup **WATER**
JUICE of ½ **LEMON**

BANANA Gobs
WITH BUTTERED-RUM FILLING

This gob was another happy accident. I had some extra Buttered-Rum Filling, just waiting to be put to tasty use, when I spied some bananas on the kitchen counter. Bananas and rum: a perfect tropical combo. If you like, you can swap the buttermilk in the batter for coconut milk to give this gob an even more exotic edge, but be aware that it will change the consistency ever so slightly and produce a more cookie-like gob.

1. Preheat the oven to 350°F. Line three 8-by-13-inch cookie sheets with parchment paper.

2. In a large bowl, sift together the flour, baking powder, baking soda, and salt. Whisk the dry ingredients until they're evenly distributed.

3. In another large bowl, cream the sugar and butter with a mixer on medium speed. Add the egg yolks to the creamed ingredients, and mix on medium. Then add the egg whites and vanilla, and mix on medium-high until the mixture looks like dense pudding. Add the banana pulp and blend on high until the mixture is fluffy.

4. Alternate adding the dry ingredients and the buttermilk and sour cream to the egg mixture, mixing on medium speed after each addition.

5. Using a tablespoon or pastry bag, drop 1½-inch rounds of batter on the prepared cookie sheets, leaving 1 inch between each round. Bake them approximately 8 minutes, or until the gob domes have risen. Remove the gobs to a wire rack to cool.

1. Follow the filling recipe for Spiced Pumpkin Gobs with Buttered-Rum Filling, page 60.

1. Place the banana, sugar, vanilla bean, cinnamon stick, and water in a medium saucepan. Bring the liquid to a boil over medium heat, stirring to dissolve the sugar.

2. Reduce the heat to low and simmer, stirring occasionally, until the banana turns to mush (approximately 10 minutes; it will reduce quickly).

3. Strain the liquid, reserving it for the gob filling.

4. Place the banana pulp in separate bowl, mix in the sour cream, and reserve it for the gob batter.

FOR THE **BATTER**

- **4 cups plus 2 tablespoons all-purpose FLOUR**
- **½ teaspoon BAKING POWDER**
- **1½ teaspoons BAKING SODA**
- **1 teaspoon SALT**
- **2 cups SUGAR, sifted**
- **8 tablespoons UNSALTED BUTTER, softened, cut in ½-inch cubes**
- **2 EGGS, separated, at room temperature**
- **1 teaspoon VANILLA EXTRACT**
- **½ cup plus 1 tablespoon BANANA PULP (recipe follows)**
- **1 cup BUTTERMILK, at room temperature (or coconut milk)**
- **1 tablespoon of SOUR CREAM**

FOR THE **FILLING**

See ingredients, page 60

FOR THE

BANANA PULP

- **2 whole BANANAS sliced, preferably from overripe fruit**
- **½ cup SUGAR**
- **1 VANILLA BEAN, split, with seeds scraped**
- **1 CINNAMON STICK**
- **½ cup WATER**
- **2 tablespoons SOUR CREAM**

HORCHATA
GOBS WITH Almond Lime Filling

Assimilation and adaptation are two of the most defining characteristics of American kitchens. When I first moved to San Francisco, I encountered horchata-flavored Popsicles and cupcakes long before I even had my first sip of the traditional almond-and-lime-laced drink from Mexico. Everything about the beverage appealed to me—especially the way the clean lime notes balanced the devilishness of the cinnamon—and I wanted to try my own horchata creation. I could see the components of the gob as perfect conduits for the popular drink's flavors.

Since the nuts and rice in the homemade horchata need to soak for 24 hours, you can make this recipe a little easier by using canned horchata—just eliminate the extra buttermilk. If you have the time, though, following my instructions for the homemade version will give you a truly unique experience in both flavor and texture. Left a little rough and grainy, the rice in the horchata will mix with the flour to create a dense yet airy cake.

1. Preheat the oven to 350°F. Line three 8-by-13-inch cookie sheets with parchment paper.

2. In a large bowl, sift together the flour, cocoa powder, baking powder, baking soda, and salt. Whisk the dry ingredients until they're evenly distributed.

3. In another large bowl, cream the sugar and butter with a mixer on medium speed. Add the lime zest and egg yolks to the creamed ingredients, and mix on medium. Then add the egg whites, vanilla extract, and almond extract, and mix on medium-high until the mixture looks like dense pudding. Add the horchata, and mix on high.

4. Alternate adding the dry ingredients and the buttermilk to the egg mixture, mixing on medium speed after each addition. Then add the sour cream, and mix well.

5. Using a tablespoon or pastry bag, drop 1½-inch rounds of batter on the prepared cookie sheets, leaving 1 inch between each round. Bake them approximately 8 minutes, or until the gob domes have risen. Remove the gobs to a wire rack to cool.

FOR THE BATTER

- 4 cups all-purpose FLOUR
- ½ cup COCOA POWDER
- ½ teaspoon BAKING POWDER
- 1½ teaspoons BAKING SODA
- 1 teaspoon SALT
- 1¾ cups SUGAR, sifted
- 8 tablespoons UNSALTED BUTTER, softened, cut in ½-inch cubes
- 1½ tablespoons LIME ZEST
- 2 EGGS, separated, at room temperature
- ½ teaspoon VANILLA EXTRACT
- ½ teaspoon ALMOND EXTRACT
- 1 cup HORCHATA (recipe follows)
- 1 cup BUTTERMILK, at room temperature (½ cup if using canned horchata)
- 2 tablespoons SOUR CREAM

1. Cream together the butter and cream cheese with a mixer on medium speed.

2. Add the almond extract, lime zest, 1 tablespoon of lime juice and the confectioners' sugar, and beat on medium-high; scrape the bowl with a spatula to reincorporate the ingredients if necessary. Taste and add another tablespoon of lime juice if you like.

3. To frost the gobs, flip the baked gob domes over on a cookie sheet and match up pairs of similarly shaped domes. Add 1 tablespoon of filling to the flat side of an overturned dome, then place another dome on top, sandwich-style. Allow the gobs to fully set by refrigerating them on a baking sheet in the fridge for at least 1 hour. Wrap the gobs in plastic wrap to prevent them from drying out.

FOR THE FILLING

- 8 tablespoons UNSALTED BUTTER, softened, cut in ½-inch cubes
- 12 tablespoons CREAM CHEESE, cut in ½-inch cubes
- 1 tablespoon ALMOND EXTRACT
- 1 tablespoon LIME ZEST
- 2 to 3 tablespoons fresh LIME JUICE
- 2 cups CONFECTIONERS' SUGAR, sifted

NOTE: Prepare this recipe a day in advance.

1. Working in small batches of about 2 tablespoons at a time, grind the rice in a coffee mill or spice mill until it's very fine.

2. In a large bowl, combine the ground rice, almonds, cinnamon stick, vanilla bean, and lime zest. Pour in the hot water, cover the bowl, and set it aside on a countertop away from direct light or a heat source for approximately 24 hours.

3. Transfer the mixture to a blender or food processor. Process on high until it's smooth. Add the sugar and the 2 cups of cool water to the blender, and process on high.

4. Press the mixture through cheesecloth or a sieve into a bowl. It should have a smooth but slightly grainy consistency; if it's too thick, pass it through the cheesecloth or sieve at least two more times. Set the mixture aside. (If you have horchata left over from the gob batter recipe, add approximately 2 more cups of cool water to it, then blend and strain it again. It will keep as a beverage, refrigerated, for up to 2 weeks.)

FOR THE HORCHATA

- 8 tablespoons long-grain white **RICE**
- 1 **CINNAMON STICK**
- 1 cup whole **ALMONDS**
- 1 whole **VANILLA BEAN**
- **ZEST** of 1 **LIME**
- 3 cups **HOT WATER**
- 1¼ cups **SUGAR**
- 2 cups **COOL WATER**

COCONUT GOBS
WITH UBE FILLING

I was at Mitchell's Ice Cream, a San Francisco institution since 1953, when I spied a beautiful royal purple ice cream and learned that it was made from a yam known as "ube." I immediately wanted to find a way to incorporate this exotic beauty, a beloved mainstay of Filipino cooking , in my gob repertoire. Ube (pronounced OO-bay, by the way) can be found at most good Asian markets—sometimes it's fresh, but most often it's in the freezer section, so my recipe calls for the frozen yams. They give the finished filling a beautiful lavender hue.

If you want a brighter, electric purple color—like something Prince would've coveted, circa 1982—you can cheat with food dye. There are several safe, all-natural food colorings on the market.

RECIPE CONTINUES

1. Preheat the oven to 350°F. Line three 8-by-13-inch cookie sheets with parchment paper.

2. In a large bowl, sift together the flour, baking powder, baking soda, and salt. Whisk the dry ingredients until they're evenly distributed

3. In another large bowl, cream the sugar and butter with a mixer on medium speed. Add the egg yolks to the creamed ingredients, and mix on medium. Add the egg whites, vanilla, and coconut extract, and mix on medium-high until the mixture looks like dense pudding.

4. Alternate adding the dry ingredients and the coconut milk to the egg mixture, mixing on medium speed after each addition. Then add the sour cream, and mix well.

5. Using a tablespoon or pastry bag, drop 1½-inch rounds of batter on the prepared cookie sheets, leaving 1 inch between each round. Bake them approximately 8 minutes, or until the gob domes have risen. Remove the gobs to a wire rack to cool.

FOR THE BATTER

- **4 cups plus 2 tablespoons all-purpose FLOUR**
- **½ teaspoon BAKING POWDER**
- **1½ teaspoons BAKING SODA**
- **1 teaspoon SALT**
- **2 cups SUGAR, sifted**
- **8 tablespoons UNSALTED BUTTER, softened, cut in ½-inch cubes**
- **2 EGGS, separated, at room temperature**
- **½ teaspoon VANILLA EXTRACT**
- **½ teaspoon COCONUT EXTRACT**
- **1 cup unsweetened COCONUT MILK (if using canned, stir well before emptying)**
- **2 tablespoons SOUR CREAM**

1. Cream together the butter and cream cheese with a mixer on medium speed.

2. Add the vanilla, lemon juice, and confectioners' sugar, and mix on medium. Then add ½ cup of ube and beat until the mixture is fluffy; scrape the bowl with a spatula to reincorporate the ingredients if necessary. Taste and add another tablespoon of lemon juice if you like. If the filling looks like it needs more stability, add more ube.

3. To frost the gobs, flip the baked gob domes over on a cookie sheet and match up pairs of similarly shaped domes. Add 1 tablespoon of filling to the flat side of an overturned dome, then place another dome on top, sandwich-style. Allow the gobs to fully set by refrigerating them on a baking sheet for at least 1 hour. Wrap the gobs in plastic wrap to prevent them from drying out.

FOR THE FILLING

- **8 tablespoons UNSALTED BUTTER, softened, cut in ½-inch cubes**
- **12 tablespoons CREAM CHEESE, cut in ½-inch cubes**
- **1 teaspoon VANILLA EXTRACT**
- **3 to 4 tablespoons fresh LEMON JUICE**
- **1½ cups CONFECTIONERS' SUGAR, sifted**
- **½ to 1 cup UBE PUREE (recipe follows)**

1. Defrost the ube according to the package instructions. Cut the defrosted ube into 1-inch cubes, preparing enough to measure 2 cups.

2. Put the ube, sugar, lemon juice, and 1 cup of water in a saucepan. Bring the liquid to a boil.

3. Reduce the heat and simmer, stirring occasionally to mash up the ube. When a paste starts to form, remove the pan from the heat and allow the mixture to cool. If the mixture becomes too thick, add more water, one tablespoon at a time.

4. Add cooled ube mixture to a food processor and carefully puree it. If the mix becomes too starchy, add more water. Reserve the ube puree for the gob filling.

FOR THE UBE PUREE

2 cups frozen UBE

½ cup SUGAR

JUICE of 1 LEMON (approximately 3 tablespoons)

1 to 1½ cups WATER

BACON GOBS

You don't have to be a resident of San Francisco for long to learn that there are two types of people in the city: those who eat bacon and those who don't. The love of all things porcine here is so rapturous, in fact, that I can't even divide the groups into carnivore and "those who never digest animal products" categories. Not in this town! I've watched avowed vegans nervously glance over their shoulder as they furtively took bites of this gob.

The pairing of chocolate and bacon might seem odd, but in the same way that cocoa is a perfect complement to chili peppers, it makes a tasty conduit for the smoky pork goodness in this confection.

The main recipe below relies on bacon jam, which is much more subtle in flavor. The variation uses good old-fashioned bacon fat, and will give you a porky taste as big as a barnyard.

NOTE: Skillet Street Food's bacon jam can be purchased online, at http://skilletstreetfood.com/baconjam.htm, and in select stores. If you don't have access to bacon jam, use 6 tablespoons of butter and 2 tablespoons of rendered, cooked bacon fat (6 strips should do the trick depending on how fatty they are) that has been strained at least once. Cream the bacon fat along with the butter and sugar in step 3.

1. Preheat the oven to 350°F. Line three 8-by-13-inch cookie sheets with parchment paper.

2. In a large bowl, sift together the flour, cocoa powder, baking powder, baking soda, and salt. Whisk the dry ingredients until they're evenly distributed

3. In another large bowl, cream the sugar and butter with a mixer on medium speed. Add the egg yolks to the creamed ingredients, and mix on medium. Then add the egg whites and vanilla, and mix on medium-high until the mixture looks like dense pudding. Add bacon jam, and mix on high.

4. Alternate adding the dry ingredients and the buttermilk to the egg mixture, mixing on medium speed after each addition. Then add the sour cream, and mix well.

5. Using a tablespoon or pastry bag, drop 1½-inch rounds of batter on the prepared cookie sheets, leaving 1 inch between each round. Bake them approximately 8 minutes, or until the gob domes have risen. Remove the gobs to a wire rack to cool.

FOR THE **BATTER**

- **4 cups all-purpose FLOUR**
- **½ cup COCOA POWDER**
- **½ teaspoon BAKING POWDER**
- **1½ teaspoons BAKING SODA**
- **1 teaspoon SALT**
- **2 cups SUGAR, sifted**
- **8 tablespoons UNSALTED BUTTER, softened, cut in ½-inch cubes**
- **2 EGGS, separated, at room temperature**
- **1 teaspoon VANILLA EXTRACT**
- **½ cup BACON JAM, pureed**
- **1 cup BUTTERMILK, at room temperature**
- **2 to 3 tablespoons SOUR CREAM**

1. Cream together the butter and cream cheese with a mixer on medium speed.

2. Add the vanilla, 1 tablespoon of lemon juice, the maple syrup, and the confectioners' sugar, and beat on medium-high; scrape the bowl with a spatula to reincorporate the ingredients if necessary. Taste and add another tablespoon of lemon juice if you like.

3. To frost the gobs, flip the baked gob domes over on a cookie sheet and match up pairs of similarly shaped domes. Add 1 tablespoon of filling to the flat side of an overturned dome, then place another dome on top, sandwich-style. Allow the gobs to fully set by refrigerating them on baking sheet for at least 1 hour. Wrap the gobs in plastic wrap to prevent them from drying out.

FOR THE **FILLING**

- **8 tablespoons UNSALTED BUTTER, softened, cut in ½-inch cubes**
- **12 tablespoons CREAM CHEESE, cut in ½-inch cubes**
- **1 teaspoon VANILLA EXTRACT**
- **1 to 2 tablespoons fresh LEMON JUICE**
- **1 tablespoon MAPLE SYRUP**
- **2 cups CONFECTIONERS' SUGAR, sifted**

CHOCOLATE GOBS WITH Dulce de Leche FILLING

Dulce de leche is a Spanish delight made by slowly reducing milk and sugar into caramel—and I do mean slowly. The filling for this gob requires a significant time commitment on your part. If you haven't spent any quality time with your stovetop lately, this recipe will help the two of you reconnect—and I think you'll agree that it's well worth it.

You could cut corners and use canned dulce de leche, which is available at most grocery stores. But the satisfaction that comes from whiffing the buttery aroma as the milk and sugar meld turns this process into a wonderful sensory experience. And I haven't even said anything about the taste yet!

Use the best-quality vanilla extract that you can for this filling. The slight tang of cream cheese serves as an excellent base for the filling; just don't exceed the amount called for or you run the risk of overpowering the decadent flavor that you've invested so much time in making

If you choose, you can also skip the filling and slather the pure dulce de leche directly between the gob domes. You will need to make an extra batch of the caramel, though. Chill it for easier spreading. Once the gobs are constructed, keep them in the coldest part of your fridge until you're ready to serve them.

1. Preheat the oven to 350°F. Line three 8-by-13-inch cookie sheets with parchment paper.

2. In a large bowl, sift together the flour, cocoa powder, baking powder, baking soda, and salt. Whisk the dry ingredients until they're evenly distributed

3. In another large bowl, cream the sugar and butter with a mixer on medium speed. Add the egg yolks to the creamed ingredients, and mix on medium. Then add the egg whites and vanilla, and mix on medium-high until the mixture looks like dense pudding.

4. Alternate adding the dry ingredients and the buttermilk to the egg mixture, mixing on medium speed after each addition. Then add the sour cream, and mix well.

5. Using a tablespoon or pastry bag, drop 1½-inch rounds of batter on the prepared cookie sheets, leaving 1 inch between each round. Bake them approximately 8 minutes, or until the gob domes have risen. Remove the gobs to a wire rack to cool.

FOR THE BATTER

- **4 cups all-purpose FLOUR**
- **½ cup COCOA POWDER**
- **½ teaspoon BAKING POWDER**
- **1½ teaspoons BAKING SODA**
- **1 teaspoon SALT**
- **2 cups SUGAR, sifted**
- **8 tablespoons UNSALTED BUTTER, softened, cut in ½-inch cubes**
- **2 EGGS, separated, at room temperature**
- **1 teaspoon VANILLA EXTRACT**
- **1 cup BUTTERMILK**
- **2 tablespoons SOUR CREAM**

1. Cream the cream cheese with a mixer on medium speed. Slowly pour the dulce de leche into the cream cheese and mix on low speed.

2. Add 1 tablespoon of lemon juice, the vanilla, and the confectioners' sugar, and mix on medium-high speed; scrape the bowl with a spatula to reincorporate the ingredients if necessary. Beat the mixture until it's spreadable. If it's too thick, add more lemon juice, a teaspoon at a time.

3. To frost the gobs, flip the baked gob domes over on a cookie sheet and match up pairs of similarly shaped domes. Add 1 tablespoon of filling to the flat side of an overturned dome, then place another dome on top, sandwich-style. Allow the gobs to fully set by refrigerating them on a baking sheet for at least 1 hour. Wrap the gobs in plastic wrap to prevent them from drying out.

FOR THE FILLING

- **12 tablespoons CREAM CHEESE, cut in ½-inch cubes**
- **1½ cups DULCE DE LECHE (recipe follows)**
- **1 to 2 tablespoons fresh LEMON JUICE**
- **1 tablespoon VANILLA EXTRACT**
- **1 cup CONFECTIONERS' SUGAR, sifted**

1. In a medium saucepan, bring the milk and sugar to a near boil, stirring occasionally to dissolve the sugar.

2. While the milk is heating, split the vanilla bean lengthwise and, with the tip of a knife, scrape the seeds out of the pod, and add the pod and seeds to the saucepan.

3. When the mixture is almost boiling, add the baking soda. Reduce the heat to low and cook the mixture, stirring every few minutes, for 90 minutes, or until the mixture reduces by more than half. As the milk reduces, foam will form on top of the mixture and along the sides of pot; do not stir this foam back into the mix. Allow to simmer on low for up to an additional 60 minutes, stirring frequently, to be sure mixture reduces by half.

NOTE: I allow the sugar to brown a little on the bottom of the pot. It makes for a rich color and a slightly smoky caramel flavor, and the browned bits will be strained out.

4. Once the mixture is reduced, remove the vanilla bean pod. Strain the liquid, allow it to cool, and reserve it for the gob filling. You should have just under 2 cups.

FOR THE

DULCE DE LECHE

4 cups WHOLE MILK

1½ cups plus 1 tablespoon SUGAR

1 VANILLA BEAN

½ teaspoon BAKING SODA

ORANGE GOBS
WITH ORANGE DULCE DE LECHE FILLING

I love the combination of orange and caramel, so it was only a matter of time—and milk, sugar, and orange zest—before I dressed up a gob with Orange Dulce de Leche Filling. The gob batter here gets a sunny burst from orange extract *and* orange zest, which adds texture and bits of color.

I enjoy serving this gob cold because the creamy orange flavor and texture of the filling remind me of an orange Creamsicle. I've also used this filling—with delicious results—sandwiched between the gobs from my S.F. Chocolate Vanilla Gobs recipe, and also the Chocolate Ancho.

NOTE: When you peel the orange for the dulce de leche, avoid getting too much of the white pith, which will add a slight bitterness to your cream. You can remove most of the orange peel from the caramel at the 90-minute mark.

RECIPE CONTINUES

1. Preheat the oven to 350°F. Line three 8-by-13-inch cookie sheets with parchment paper.

2. In a large bowl, sift together the flour, baking powder, baking soda, and salt. Whisk the dry ingredients until they're evenly distributed.

3. In another large bowl, cream the sugar and butter with a mixer on medium speed. Add the egg yolks to the creamed ingredients, and mix on medium. Add the egg whites, orange zest, vanilla, and orange extract, and mix on medium-high until the mixture looks like dense pudding.

4. Alternate adding the dry ingredients and the buttermilk to the egg mixture, mixing on medium speed after each addition. Then add the sour cream, and mix well.

5. Using a tablespoon or pastry bag, drop 1½-inch rounds of batter on the prepared cookie sheets, leaving 1 inch between each round. Bake them approximately 8 minutes, or until the gob domes have risen. Remove the gobs to a wire rack to cool.

FOR THE BATTER

- **4 cups plus 2 tablespoons** all-purpose **FLOUR**
- **½ teaspoon BAKING POWDER**
- **1½ teaspoons BAKING SODA**
- **1 teaspoon SALT**
- **2 cups SUGAR**, sifted
- **8 tablespoons UNSALTED BUTTER**, softened, cut in ½-inch cubes
- **2 EGGS**, separated, at room temperature
- **2 tablespoons ORANGE ZEST**
- **½ teaspoon VANILLA EXTRACT**
- **½ teaspoon ORANGE EXTRACT**
- **1 cup BUTTERMILK**, at room temperature
- **2 tablespoons SOUR CREAM**

1. Cream the cream cheese with a mixer on medium speed. Slowly pour the dulce de leche into the cream cheese, and mix on low speed.

2. Add 1 tablespoon of lemon juice, the vanilla, and the confectioners' sugar, and beat on medium-high speed; scrape the bowl with a spatula to reincorporate the ingredients if necessary. Beat the mixture until it's spreadable. If it's too thick, add more lemon juice, a teaspoon at a time.

3. To frost the gobs, flip the baked gob domes over on a cookie sheet and match up pairs of similarly shaped domes. Add 1 tablespoon of filling to the flat side of an overturned dome, then place another dome on top, sandwich-style. Allow the gobs to fully set by refrigerating them on a baking sheet for at least 1 hour. Wrap the gobs in plastic wrap to prevent them from drying out.

FOR THE FILLING

- **12 tablespoons CREAM CHEESE**, cut in ½-inch cubes
- **1½ cups ORANGE DULCE DE LECHE** (recipe follows)
- **1 to 2 tablespoons fresh LEMON JUICE**
- **1 tablespoon VANILLA EXTRACT**
- **1 cup CONFECTIONERS' SUGAR**, sifted

1. Place the milk, sugar, and orange peel in a medium saucepan. Bring the liquid to a near boil, stirring occasionally to dissolve the sugar.

2. Add the baking soda, reduce the heat to low, and cook the mixture, stirring every few minutes, for 90 minutes, or until the mixture reduces by more than half. Do not stir in the foam. It will accumulate and thicken on the sides of the pot as you stir. This is to be expected. Do not reincorporate back into milk. After 30 minutes, taste for bitterness. Check at 60 minutes and then at 90 again. If orange is turning bitter at any point, remove peels immediately. At the 2-hour point remove all peels. Allow to simmer for another 30 minutes to reduce.

NOTE: I allow the sugar to brown a little on the bottom of the pot. It makes for a rich color and slightly smoky caramel flavor, and the browned bits will be strained out.

3. Once the mixture is reduced, strain the liquid, allow it to cool, and reserve it for the gob filling. You should have just under 2 cups.

FOR THE

ORANGE DULCE DE LECHE

4 cups WHOLE MILK

1½ cups plus 1 tablespoon SUGAR

Peel of 1 ORANGE, (white pith removed) cut into 4 strips

½ teaspoon BAKING SODA

CHOCOLATE, ORANGE, HAZELNUT Gobs

I like to think of this gob as a baked version of Toblerone's Chocolate Orange, which hits the shelves around Christmas—but this one's sauced up with hazelnut liqueur. I use Frangelico in the filling, and everything about this gob's flavor and aroma is so festive that I am immediately transported to the holiday season, at least in my mind, every time I bake it.

The orange extract and hazelnut liqueur can stand up to even the most muscled-up chocolate flavor, but using a mild cocoa powder will make you think you're having a smooth, chocolaty digestif! I know I almost insist on using Green & Black's organic cocoa throughout this text, but this is one recipe where I'll make allowances. So go ahead and reach for the Hershey's. I'm not looking.

1. Preheat the oven to 350°F. Line three 8-by-13-inch cookie sheets with parchment paper.

2. In a large bowl, sift together the flour, cocoa powder, baking powder, baking soda, and salt. Whisk the dry ingredients until they're evenly distributed

3. In another large bowl, cream the sugar and butter with a mixer on medium speed. Add the egg yolks to the creamed ingredients, and mix on medium. Then add the egg whites, orange zest, vanilla, and orange extract, and mix on medium-high until the mixture looks like dense pudding.

4. Alternate adding the dry ingredients and the buttermilk to the egg mixture, mixing on medium speed after each addition. Mix well.

5. Using a tablespoon or pastry bag, drop 1½-inch rounds of batter on the prepared cookie sheets, leaving 1 inch between each round. Bake them approximately 8 minutes, or until the gob domes have risen. Remove the gobs to a wire rack to cool.

FOR THE BATTER

- 4 cups all-purpose FLOUR
- ½ cup COCOA POWDER
- ½ teaspoon BAKING POWDER
- 1½ teaspoons BAKING SODA
- 1 teaspoon SALT
- 2 cups SUGAR, sifted
- 8 tablespoons UNSALTED BUTTER, softened, cut in ½-inch cubes
- 2 EGGS, separated, at room temperature
- 3 tablespoons ORANGE ZEST
- ½ teaspoon VANILLA EXTRACT
- ½ teaspoon ORANGE EXTRACT
- 1 cup BUTTERMILK
- 2 tablespoons SOUR CREAM

1. Cream together the butter and cream cheese with a mixer on medium speed.

2. Add the Frangelico, vanilla, lemon juice, and confectioners' sugar, and mix on medium-high; scrape the bowl with a spatula to reincorporate the ingredients if necessary.

3. To frost the gobs, flip the baked gob domes over on a cookie sheet and match up pairs of similarly shaped domes. Add 1 tablespoon of filling to the flat side of an overturned dome, then place another dome on top, sandwich-style. Allow the gobs to fully set by refrigerating them on a baking sheet for at least 1 hour. Wrap the gobs in plastic wrap to prevent them from drying out.

FOR THE FILLING

- 8 tablespoons UNSALTED BUTTER, softened, cut in ½-inch cubes
- 12 tablespoons CREAM CHEESE, cut in ½-inch cubes
- 3 tablespoons FRANGELICO HAZELNUT LIQUEUR
- 1 tablespoon VANILLA EXTRACT
- 1 tablespoon LEMON JUICE
- 2 cup CONFECTIONERS' SUGAR, sifted

ALAMEDA FREE LIBRARY

CHOCOLATE CHOCOLATE CHOCOLATE GOBS

For the chocolate-obsessed, what could induce more flavor lust than a chocolate-covered chocolate-frosted chocolate gob? Even the pictures of the chocolate-covered half domes that I posted on the Web created a stir. Why? Because chocolate is one of those foods that provides the total sensory experience. And in this gob, you have a lot to experience—the sheen of the glaçage, the moist mouthfeel, the rich smell of the cocoa, and of course, the taste-bud blowing experience of all of that chocolate in one place. Oh, your lucky, lucky mouth.

These gobs are best left unwrapped, because the glaçage-covered domes will stick to any packaging. Instead, I recommend storing them in an airtight container.

1. Preheat the oven to 350°F. Line three 8-by-13-inch cookie sheets with parchment paper.

2. In a large bowl, sift together the flour, cocoa powder, baking powder, baking soda, and salt. Whisk the dry ingredients until they're evenly distributed

3. In another large bowl, cream the sugar and butter with a mixer on medium speed. Add the egg yolks to the creamed ingredients, and mix on medium. Then add the egg whites and vanilla, and mix on medium-high until the mixture looks like dense pudding.

4. Alternate adding the dry ingredients and the buttermilk to the egg mixture, mixing on medium speed after each addition. Then add the sour cream, and mix well.

5. Using a tablespoon or pastry bag, drop 1½-inch rounds of batter on the prepared cookie sheets, leaving 1 inch between each round. Bake them approximately 8 minutes, or until the gob domes have risen. Remove the gobs to a wire rack to cool.

FOR THE BATTER

- 4 cups all-purpose FLOUR
- ½ cup COCOA POWDER
- ½ teaspoon BAKING POWDER
- 1½ teaspoons BAKING SODA
- 1 teaspoon SALT
- 2 cups SUGAR, sifted
- 8 tablespoons UNSALTED BUTTER, softened, cut in ½-inch cubes
- 2 EGGS, separated, at room temperature
- 1 teaspoon VANILLA EXTRACT
- 1 cup BUTTERMILK, at room temperature
- 2 tablespoons SOUR CREAM

1. Cream together the butter and cream cheese with a mixer on medium speed. Add the vanilla and lemon juice to the creamed mixture, and blend on medium-high.

2. In a separate bowl, sift the cocoa powder in with confectioners' sugar, and whisk to mix well.

3. Add the confectioner's sugar and cocoa powder mixture to the creamed ingredients, and mix on medium-high; scrape the bowl with a spatula to reincorporate the ingredients if necessary. Add 1 tablespoon of sour cream, and beat until the filling resembles whipped cream. If the filling is dry, beat in another tablespoon of sour cream.

FOR THE FILLING

- 8 tablespoons BUTTER, cut in ½-inch cubes
- 12 tablespoons CREAM CHEESE, cut in ½-inch cubes
- 2 tablespoons VANILLA EXTRACT
- 1 tablespoon fresh LEMON JUICE
- ¼ cup COCOA POWDER
- 1¾ cup CONFECTIONERS' SUGAR, sifted
- 1 to 2 tablespoons SOUR CREAM

1. Chop the chocolate bar into ¼-inch pieces, and place the pieces in a heat-resistant bowl.

2. Heat the heavy cream on medium until it boils. Immediately remove it from the heat, and pour it over the chocolate pieces. Stir quickly to melt the chocolate evenly.

3. Add 2 tablespoons of butter to the chocolate-and-cream mixture, and stir until it's evenly distributed. Take a ladle, scoop out some of the mixture, and drizzle it back into the bowl; if it doesn't stream easily, quickly add another tablespoon of butter. Be careful to incorporate all the butter so it doesn't leave any telltale streaks of white and yellow in your glaçage.

4. Set half the unfrosted gob domes on a wire rack with parchment paper underneath to catch the chocolate drips. Drizzle the glaçage over the gob domes. To set the glaçage, place the gob domes on a baking sheet in the coolest part of the fridge.

5. When chocolate is firm on gob domes, remove from fridge. Working quickly, place 1 tablespoon of filling on the domes that are not chocolate coated, placing a glacage-covered dome on top of each. Because these gobs will be difficult to wrap individually, place them in rows in tightly covered plastic containers.

FOR THE GLAÇAGE

- **6 ounces CHOCOLATE, chopped** preferably Green & Black's organic or best quality semi sweet dark chocolate
- **¾ cup HEAVY CREAM**
- **2 to 3 tablespoons UNSALTED BUTTER, cut in small squares**

BANANA SPLIT GOBS

Did you know that nearly all the ingredients in a banana split are considered aphrodisiacs? It's true. That little fact helped add some spark to my first collection of Valentine's Day gobs. Besides, the February farmer's markets don't have a lot of sources of inspiration. And since I take great pride in the fact that Gobba Gobba Hey relies on seasonal and local ingredients, I needed to look elsewhere for cues.

I wrestled with issues of integrity the first time I baked with ingredients that definitely didn't come off any trees in my vicinity in midwinter. But I've tried to stay as true to my mission as possible on this gob by using organic or sustainably grown bananas and organic dried cherries. If you want to go all the way with the banana split concept, you can sprinkle finely chopped walnuts over the glaçage and even add a spiral of the filling on top.

RECIPE CONTINUES

1. Preheat the oven to 350°F. Line three 8-by-13-inch cookie sheets with parchment paper.

2. In a large bowl, sift together the flour, cocoa powder, baking powder, baking soda, and salt. Whisk the dry ingredients until they're evenly distributed.

3. In another large bowl, cream the sugar and butter with a mixer on medium speed. Add the egg yolks to the creamed ingredients, and mix on medium. Then add the egg whites and vanilla, and mix on medium-high until the mixture looks like dense pudding. Add the banana pulp and mix on high until it's incorporated.

4. Alternate adding the dry ingredients and the buttermilk to the egg mixture, mixing on medium speed after each addition. Mix well.

5. Using a tablespoon or pastry bag, drop 1½-inch rounds of batter on the prepared cookie sheets, leaving 1 inch between each round. Bake them approximately 8 minutes, or until the gob domes have risen. Remove the gobs to a wire rack to cool.

1. Cream together the butter and cream cheese with a mixer on medium speed.

2. Add the cherry syrup, vanilla, and lemon juice, and confectioners' sugar. Beat on medium-high until the filling forms peaks; scrape the bowl to reincorporate the ingredients if necessary.

3. Set the filling in the fridge until ready to fill the glaçage-covered gob domes.

1. Follow the glaçage instructions on page 104 for finishing the banana split gobs.

FOR THE BATTER

- 4 cups all-purpose FLOUR
- ½ cup COCOA POWDER
- ½ teaspoon BAKING POWDER
- 1½ teaspoons BAKING SODA
- 1 teaspoon SALT
- 2 cups SUGAR, sifted
- 8 tablespoons UNSALTED BUTTER, softened, cut in ½-inch cubes
- 2 EGGS, separated, at room temperature
- 1 teaspoon VANILLA EXTRACT
- ½ cup BANANA PULP (see Banana Gobs recipe, page 85)
- 1 cup BUTTERMILK, at room temperature
- 2 to 3 tablespoons SOUR CREAM

FOR THE FILLING

- 8 tablespoons BUTTER, softened, cut in ½-inch cubes
- 12 tablespoons CREAM CHEESE, cut in ½-inch cubes
- 3 to 4 tablespoons CHERRY SYRUP (recipe follows)
- 1 teaspoon VANILLA EXTRACT
- 1 to 2 tablespoon fresh LEMON JUICE
- 2 cup CONFECTIONERS' SUGAR, sifted

FOR THE GLAÇAGE

See ingredients, page 104

1. Place the dried cherries, sugar, and water in a medium saucepan. Split the vanilla bean so the seeds can easily fall out, and add the whole bean to the saucepan. Let the pan sit for 10 minutes for the cherries to absorb the water.

2. Bring the liquid to a boil over medium heat, stirring to dissolve the sugar.

3. Reduce the heat to low and simmer, stirring occasionally, for approximately 10 minutes. The liquid will be a deep, rich burgundy that easily coats the back of a spoon.

4. Strain the syrup, reserving it for the filling; discard the cherries.

FOR THE

CHERRY SYRUP

1 cup **DRIED CHERRIES (in winter, many stores sell several varieties together; experiment as your tastes dictate)**

½ cup **SUGAR**

1 cup **WATER**

1 **VANILLA BEAN**

CHOCOLATE GOBS
WITH Peanut Butter FILLING

I love chocolate peanut butter cups, and I especially love chocolate peanut butter cup cookies—that 1970s holiday standard with the slightly melted chocolate candy sitting in a cozy pillow of peanut butter cookie dough. The mere thought of them makes me giddy. And hungry! This is the gob version of those—but without the prepackaged candies.

NOTE: It's been said that you need to use a mass-market peanut butter for the filling to set properly. Don't believe it. It's true that pure, freshly ground peanut butter will give you a difficult time, but I recommend using a good organic peanut butter that has not been hydrogenated. The cream cheese here serves as a sturdy base for your gob filling, but it can also be overpowering, so bring out the earthy goodness of the peanut butter's flavor by adding fresh-squeezed lemon juice and the best-quality vanilla extract available.

1. Preheat the oven to 350°F. Line three 8-by-13-inch cookie sheets with parchment paper.

2. In a large bowl, sift together the flour, cocoa powder, baking powder, baking soda, and salt. Whisk the dry ingredients until they're evenly distributed.

3. In another large bowl, cream the sugar and butter with a mixer on medium speed. Add the egg yolks to the creamed ingredients, and mix on medium. Then add the egg whites and vanilla, and mix on medium-high until the mixture looks like dense pudding.

4. Alternate adding the dry ingredients and the buttermilk to the egg mixture, mixing on medium speed after each addition. Then add the sour cream, and mix well.

5. Using a tablespoon or pastry bag, drop 1½-inch rounds of batter on the prepared cookie sheets, leaving 1 inch between each round. Bake them approximately 8 minutes, or until the gob domes have risen. Remove the gobs to a wire rack to cool.

1. Cream the cream cheese with a mixer on medium.

2. Adding peanut butter, half cup at a time, begin to mix. Add all vanilla followed by the first tablespoon of lemon juice, watching to make sure the filling doesn't become too thick. Add the remaining lemon juice.

3. Add the confectioner's sugar, and mix on medium-high until peaks form; scrape the bowl to reincorporate the ingredients if necessary.

4. To frost the gobs, flip the baked gob domes over on a cookie sheet and match up pairs of similarly shaped domes. Add 1 tablespoon of filling to the flat side of an overturned dome, then place another dome on top, sandwich-style. Allow the gobs to fully set by refrigerating them on a baking sheet for at least 1 hour. Wrap the gobs in plastic wrap to prevent them from drying out.

FOR THE BATTER

- **4 cups all-purpose FLOUR**
- **½ cup COCOA POWDER**
- **½ teaspoon BAKING POWDER**
- **1½ teaspoons BAKING SODA**
- **1 teaspoon SALT**
- **2 cups SUGAR, sifted**
- **8 tablespoons UNSALTED BUTTER, softened, cut in ½-inch cubes**
- **2 EGGS, separated, at room temperature**
- **1 teaspoon VANILLA EXTRACT**
- **1 cup BUTTERMILK, at room temperature**
- **2 tablespoons SOUR CREAM**

FOR THE FILLING

- **12 tablespoons CREAM CHEESE, cut in ½-inch cubes**
- **1½ cups good-quality PEANUT BUTTER (preferably organic)**
- **2 tablespoons VANILLA EXTRACT**
- **1 to 2 tablespoons fresh LEMON JUICE**
- **1 cup CONFECTIONERS' SUGAR, sifted**

CHOCOLATE CHOCOLATE MALT GOBS

If there was ever a flavor that was just waiting to find its way into a gob, it's malted milk. A gob even looks like a giant malted milk ball. While lacking the crunch of the candy, my Chocolate Chocolate Malt Gob has the benefit of a rich frosted center that makes me want to twist it and eat it like an Oreo!

NOTE: For an extra-special treat, coat your chocolate malt gobs with glaçage after they've been assembled. Just make sure the melted glaze is sufficiently cool, while still being loose enough to pour, so it coats the gobs without making them slide into a hot mess.

1. Preheat the oven to 350°F. Line three 8-by-13-inch cookie sheets with parchment paper.

2. In a large bowl, sift together the flour, cocoa powder, baking powder, baking soda, and salt. Whisk the dry ingredients until they're evenly distributed

3. In another large bowl, cream the sugar and butter with a mixer on medium speed. Add the egg yolks to the creamed ingredients, and mix on medium. Then add the egg whites and vanilla, and mix on medium-high until the mixture looks like dense pudding.

4. Alternate adding the dry ingredients and the buttermilk to the egg mixture, mixing on medium speed after each addition. Then add the sour cream, and mix well.

5. Using a tablespoon or pastry bag, drop 1½-inch rounds of batter on the prepared cookie sheets, leaving 1 inch between each round. Bake them approximately 8 minutes, or until the gob domes have risen. Remove the gobs to a wire rack to cool.

1. Sift together the malted milk powder, cocoa powder, and confectioners' sugar in a larger bowl.

2. Cream together the butter and cream cheese with a mixer on medium speed in a large bowl. Then slowly drizzle the heavy cream into the creamed mixture, and mix on medium low.

3. Add the dry ingredients to dairy ingredients, ¼ cup at a time, beating on medium speed after each addition until it's well integrated. If the mixture gets too thick before all the dry ingredients are added, mix in 2 tablespoons of vanilla and 1 tablespoon of lemon juice, mix on medium high, then add last of the lemon juice; otherwise, add the vanilla and lemon juice once all the dry ingredients are in.

4. To frost the gobs, flip the baked gob domes over on a cookie sheet and match up pairs of similarly shaped domes. Add 1 tablespoon of filling to the flat side of an overturned dome, then place another dome on top, sandwich-style. Allow the gobs to fully set by refrigerating them on a baking sheet for at least 1 hour. Wrap the gobs in plastic wrap to prevent them from drying out.

FOR THE **BATTER**

- 4 cups all-purpose FLOUR
- ½ cup COCOA POWDER
- ½ teaspoon BAKING POWDER
- 1½ teaspoons BAKING SODA
- 1 teaspoon SALT
- 2 cups SUGAR, sifted
- 8 tablespoons UNSALTED BUTTER, softened, cut in ½-inch cubes
- 2 EGGS, separated, at room temperature
- 1 teaspoon VANILLA EXTRACT
- 1 cup BUTTERMILK, at room temperature
- 2 tablespoons SOUR CREAM

FOR THE **FILLING**

- ½ cup MALTED MILK POWDER
- ½ cup COCOA POWDER
- 1½ cup CONFECTIONERS' SUGAR, sifted
- 8 tablespoons BUTTER, softened, cut in ½-inch cubes
- 8 tablespoons CREAM CHEESE, cut in ½-inch cubes
- ½ cup HEAVY CREAM
- 1 to 2 tablespoons VANILLA EXTRACT
- 1 to 2 tablespoons fresh LEMON JUICE

ASIAN PEAR
GOBS

There are several devout Gobba Gobba Hey followers who insist that this is their absolute favorite gob ever. And trust me, these people have eaten more gob varieties than nearly anyone else I know! The appeal lies in the simplicity of the flavor and the lightness of the texture. Choose the Husoi variety of Asian pears if you can find them. They have a sweet crispness that is remarkably clean. But what makes them really special is the way they are transformed when worked into the gob batter. If you've never baked with these gems, then you're in for a true revelation. They give a spongy texture to the gob and have a lemony note that plays well off the citrusy scent of the coriander.

1. Preheat the oven to 350°F. Line three 8-by-13-inch cookie sheets with parchment paper.

2. In a large bowl, sift together the flour, coriander, baking powder, baking soda, and salt. Whisk the dry ingredients until they're evenly distributed.

3. In another large bowl, cream the sugar and butter with a mixer on medium speed. Add the egg yolks to the creamed ingredients, and mix on medium. Then add the egg whites and vanilla, and mix on medium-high until the mixture looks like dense pudding. Add the pear pulp, and mix on medium.

4. Alternate adding the dry ingredients and the buttermilk to the egg mixture, mixing on medium speed after each addition. Then add the sour cream, and mix well.

5. Using a tablespoon or pastry bag, drop 1½-inch rounds of batter on the prepared cookie sheets, leaving 1 inch between each round. Bake them approximately 8 minutes, or until the gob domes have risen. Remove the gobs to a wire rack to cool.

FOR THE BATTER

- **4 cups plus 2 tablespoons all-purpose FLOUR**
- **1½ tablespoons GROUND CORIANDER**
- **½ teaspoon BAKING POWDER**
- **1½ teaspoons BAKING SODA**
- **1 teaspoon SALT**
- **2 cups SUGAR, sifted**
- **8 tablespoons UNSALTED BUTTER, softened, cut in ½-inch cubes**
- **2 EGGS, separated, at room temperature**
- **1 teaspoon VANILLA EXTRACT**
- **½ cup ASIAN PEAR PULP (recipe follows)**
- **1 cup BUTTERMILK, at room temperature**
- **2 tablespoons SOUR CREAM**

1. Cream together the butter and cream cheese with a mixer on medium speed.

2. Add the vanilla, 1 tablespoon of lemon juice, 2 tablespoons of Asian pear syrup, and the confectioners' sugar, and mix on medium-high until the filling resembles whipped cream; scrape the bowl with a spatula to reincorporate the ingredients if necessary. Taste and add another tablespoon of lemon juice or Asian pear syrup if you like.

3. To frost the gobs, flip the baked gob domes over on a cookie sheet and match up pairs of similarly shaped domes. Add 1 tablespoon of filling to the flat side of an overturned dome, then place another dome on top, sandwich-style. Allow the gobs to fully set by refrigerating them on a baking sheet for at least 1 hour. Wrap the gobs in plastic wrap to prevent them from drying out.

FOR THE FILLING

- **8 tablespoons BUTTER, softened, cut in ½-inch cubes**
- **12 tablespoons CREAM CHEESE, cut in ½-inch cubes**
- **1 teaspoon VANILLA EXTRACT**
- **1 to 2 tablespoons fresh LEMON JUICE**
- **2 to 3 tablespoons ASIAN PEAR SYRUP (recipe follows)**
- **2 cup CONFECTIONERS' SUGAR, sifted**

1. Place the pears and their skins, the sugar, lemon juice, and water in a saucepan. Bring the liquid to a boil over medium heat, stirring to dissolve the sugar.

2. Reduce the heat to low and cook, stirring occasionally, until half of the water has been absorbed (approximately 10 minutes).

3. Remove the peels and strain the pears, reserving the pulp for the gob batter and the syrup for the gob filling.

FOR THE

ASIAN PEAR PULP AND SYRUP

4 **ASIAN PEARS**, preferably Husoi, peeled, cored, and coarsely chopped, with peels reserved (about 2 cups)

½ cup **SUGAR**

JUICE of ½ **LEMON**

½ cup **WATER**

UBE COCONUT GOBS

I kept coming back to the beautiful purple ube after baking my Coconut Gobs with Ube Filling (page 89), trying to find a way to incorporate the yam into the gob batter. I spent hours boiling down chunks of ube into pulp, but I got nowhere. Finally, I consulted with Ed Chui, sous-chef and half of the Filipino food cart Adobo Hobo. The Adobo Hobo serves a delicious ube cupcake. Ed shared their secret: dehydrated ube powder. Genius! You can find the powder at most Asian specialty markets, and it works like a dream.

RECIPE CONTINUES

1. Preheat the oven to 350°F. Line three 8-by-13-inch cookie sheets with parchment paper.

2. In a large bowl, sift together the flour, baking powder, baking soda, and salt. Whisk the dry ingredients until they're evenly distributed.

3. In another large bowl, cream the sugar and butter with a mixer on medium speed. Add the egg yolks to the creamed ingredients, and mix on medium. Then add the egg whites and vanilla, and mix on medium-high until the mixture looks like dense pudding. Add the ube paste, and mix on high.

4. Alternate adding the dry ingredients and the buttermilk to the egg mixture, mixing on medium speed after each addition. Add 2 tablespoons of sour cream, mix well. If batter appears too thick, add 1 additional tablespoon of sour cream and mix well again, up to a total of 4 tablespoons if needed.

5. Using a tablespoon or pastry bag, drop 1½-inch rounds of batter on the prepared cookie sheets, leaving 1 inch between each round. Bake them approximately 8 minutes, or until the gob domes have risen. Remove the gobs to a wire rack to cool.

1. Cream together the butter and cream cheese with a mixer on medium speed.

2. Add the vanilla, coconut extract, 3 tablespoons lime juice, and confectioners' sugar, and mix on medium until the mixture is fluffy; scrape the bowl with a spatula to reincorporate the ingredients if necessary. Add more lime juice if needed.

3. To frost the gobs, flip the baked gob domes over on a cookie sheet and match up pairs of similarly shaped domes. Add 1 tablespoon of filling to the flat side of an overturned dome, then place another dome on top, sandwich-style. Allow the gobs to fully set by refrigerating them on a baking sheet for at least 1 hour. Wrap the gobs in plastic wrap to prevent them from drying out.

FOR THE BATTER

- **4 cups plus 2 tablespoons** all-purpose **FLOUR**
- **½ teaspoon BAKING POWDER**
- **1½ teaspoons BAKING SODA**
- **1 teaspoon SALT**
- **2 cups SUGAR**, sifted
- **8 tablespoons UNSALTED BUTTER**, softened, cut in ½-inch cubes
- **2 EGGS**, separated, at room temperature
- **1 teaspoon VANILLA EXTRACT**
- **1 cup BUTTERMILK**, at room temperature
- **½ cup UBE PASTE** (recipe follows)
- **2 to 4 tablespoons SOUR CREAM**

FOR THE FILLING

- **8 tablespoons UNSALTED BUTTER**
- **12 tablespoons CREAM CHEESE**, cut in ½-inch cubes
- **1 teaspoon VANILLA EXTRACT**
- **1 teaspoon COCONUT EXTRACT**
- **3 to 4 tablespoons fresh LIME JUICE**
- **2 cups CONFECTIONERS' SUGAR**, sifted

1. Put the ube powder and sugar in a small bowl, and whisk to combine them.

2. Transfer the ube powder and sugar mixture to large saucepan. Add the condensed milk, coconut milk, and 2 cups of water, and stir to combine.

3. Cook the mixture over low heat, stirring occasionally. The ube will start to coagulate quickly, so add more water as needed. Cook to desired consistency (about 20 minutes). The resulting paste will look like gritty whipped potatoes.

Remove the pan from the heat and allow the mixture to cool. Reserve the ube for the gob batter.

NOTE: One can of condensed milk is approximately 14 ounces, or 1¾ cups. You need all of that for this recipe as the ube powder requires a lot of moisture to rehydrate.

FOR THE UBE PASTE

½ cup **DEHYDRATED UBE POWDER**
(about 1 4-ounce package)

½ cup **SUGAR**

1 can **CONDENSED MILK**

12 ounces **COCONUT MILK**
(if using canned, stir well before emptying)

2 to 4 cups **WATER**

ZUCCHINI
Gobs WITH Lemon-Ginger FILLING

My parents' backyard garden not only supplied herbs and vegetables for our nightly dinner table during the growing season; it also filled our family's pantry in the winter months long after the harvest. The most prolific producer was the zucchini—a very industrious squash.

After exhausting every recipe for preparing them fresh, my mom turned her attention toward canning them. By the time that task was done, the squash remaining on the vines had grown to a size that would've classified them as weapons. These squash were grated and turned into zucchini "crab" cakes and used to bulk up and moisten every other kind of cake—a use that might be one of the strongest single influences in my own kitchen.

I set out to bake a zucchini gob that would make my parents proud. With its visible shreds of green and yellow, everything about this gob is delightfully fresh.

If you want to skip making the lemon-ginger syrup for this filling, you can substitute an equal amount of straight lemon juice. But the syrup lends a silky texture that makes this gob's mouthfeel all the more enticing.

1. Preheat the oven to 350°F. Line three 8-by-13-inch cookie sheets with parchment paper.

2. In a large bowl, sift together the flour, baking powder, baking soda, and salt. Whisk the dry ingredients until they're evenly distributed.

3. In another large bowl, cream the sugar and butter with a mixer on medium speed. Add the egg yolks to the creamed ingredients, and mix on medium. Then add the egg whites and vanilla, and mix on medium-high until the mixture looks like dense pudding. Add the zucchini, ginger, and lemon zest, and mix on high.

4. Alternate adding the dry ingredients and the buttermilk to the egg mixture, mixing on medium speed after each addition. Then add the sour cream, and mix well.

5. Using a tablespoon or pastry bag, drop 1 ½-inch rounds of batter on the prepared cookie sheets, leaving 1 inch between each round. Bake them approximately 8 minutes, or until the gob domes have risen. Remove the gobs to a wire rack to cool.

FOR THE BATTER

- **4 cups plus 2 tablespoons** all-purpose **FLOUR**
- **½ teaspoon BAKING POWDER**
- **1½ teaspoons BAKING SODA**
- **1 teaspoon SALT**
- **2 cups SUGAR**, sifted
- **8 tablespoons UNSALTED BUTTER**, softened, cut in ½-inch cubes
- **2 EGGS**, separated, at room temperature
- **1 teaspoon VANILLA EXTRACT**
- **½ cup grated ZUCCHINI**
- **1 tablespoon** peeled and grated fresh **GINGER**
- **1 tablespoon LEMON ZEST**
- **1 cup BUTTERMILK**, at room temperature
- **2 tablespoons SOUR CREAM**

1. Cream together the butter and cream cheese with a mixer on medium speed.

2. Add the vanilla, lemon juice, 3 tablespoons of lemon-ginger syrup, and the confectioners' sugar, and beat on medium until the mixture is fluffy; scrape the bowl with a spatula to reincorporate the ingredients if necessary. Taste and add another tablespoon of lemon-ginger syrup if you like.

3. To frost the gobs, flip the baked gob domes over on a cookie sheet and match up pairs of similarly shaped domes. Add 1 tablespoon of filling to the flat side of an overturned dome, then place another dome on top, sandwich-style. Allow the gobs to fully set by refrigerating them on a baking sheet for at least 1 hour. Wrap the gobs in plastic wrap to prevent them from drying out.

FOR THE FILLING

- **8 tablespoons UNSALTED BUTTER**, softened, cut in ½-inch cubes
- **12 tablespoons CREAM CHEESE**, cut in ½-inch cubes
- **1 teaspoon VANILLA EXTRACT**
- **1 teaspoon LEMON JUICE**
- **3 to 4 tablespoons LEMON-GINGER SYRUP** (recipe follows)
- **2 cups CONFECTIONERS' SUGAR**, sifted

1. Place the lemon juice, ginger, sugar, and water in small saucepan. Bring the liquid to a boil over medium heat, stirring to dissolve the sugar.

2. Reduce the heat and simmer on low for 10 minutes.

3. Remove the pan from the heat and and set it aside, covered, to let the syrup steep for at least 20 minutes.

4. Strain out the ginger and reserve the syrup for the gob filling. The syrup will keep in the refrigerator for 1 month. The leftover syrup can be used in cocktails.

FOR THE

LEMON-GINGER SYRUP

JUICE of 2 LEMONS

2 tablespoons fresh GINGER, coarsely chopped

½ cup SUGAR

1 cup WATER

COCONUT GOBS WITH Rhubarb FILLING

I love rhubarb, and I missed my chance to create a gob with it during Gobba Gobba Hey's first spring. So when the first crop of these stalks pushed their way out of the ground and into the local farmer's market the following year, I practically ran to buy a supply.

Rhubarb is often paired with strawberries in desserts, but I wanted to make something simple, something that allowed the unique sweet-tart flavor of the rhubarb to stand on its own.

The syrup for the rhubarb filling beautifully distills the rhubarb's ruby red color. The flavor is a little earthy yet clean with the right balance—naturally sweet yet properly sour—and it has a crispness that reminds me of the snap of the fresh stalks. A dollop of crème fraîche in the filling accents the inherent tartness in the rhubarb without overpowering the overall flavor, and the filling pairs perfectly with the coconut flavor in the gob cake.

RECIPE CONTINUES

1. Preheat the oven to 350°F. Line three 8-by-13-inch cookie sheets with parchment paper.

2. In a large bowl, sift together the flour, baking powder, baking soda, and salt. Whisk the dry ingredients until they're evenly distributed.

3. In another large bowl, cream the sugar and butter with a mixer on medium speed. Add the egg yolks to the creamed ingredients, and mix on medium. Then add the egg whites and vanilla, and mix on medium-high until the mixture looks like dense pudding.

4. Alternate adding the dry ingredients, the buttermilk, and the coconut milk to the egg mixture, mixing on medium speed after each addition.

5. Using a tablespoon or pastry bag, drop 1½-inch rounds of batter on the prepared cookie sheets, leaving 1 inch between each round. Bake them approximately 8 minutes, or until the gob domes have risen. Remove the gobs to a wire rack to cool.

FOR THE **BATTER**

- **4 cups plus 2 tablespoons all-purpose FLOUR**
- **½ teaspoon BAKING POWDER**
- **1½ teaspoons BAKING SODA**
- **1 teaspoon SALT**
- **2 cups SUGAR, sifted**
- **8 tablespoons UNSALTED BUTTER, softened, cut in ½-inch cubes**
- **2 EGGS, separated, at room temperature**
- **1 teaspoon VANILLA EXTRACT**
- **½ cup BUTTERMILK, at room temperature**
- **½ cup COCONUT MILK, thoroughly stirred**

1. Cream together the butter and cream cheese with a mixer on medium speed.

2. Add the vanilla, crème fraîche, 1 teaspoon of lemon juice, 3 tablespoons of rhubarb syrup, and the confectioner's sugar, and beat on medium-high speed; scrape the bowl with a spatula to reincorporate the ingredients if necessary. Taste and add another teaspoon of lemon juice or tablespoon of rhubarb syrup if you like.

3. To frost the gobs, flip the baked gob domes over on a cookie sheet and match up pairs of similarly shaped domes. Add 1 tablespoon of filling to the flat side of an overturned dome, then place another dome on top, sandwich-style. Allow the gobs to fully set by refrigerating them on a baking sheet for at least 1 hour. Wrap the gobs in plastic wrap to prevent them from drying out.

FOR THE **FILLING**

- **8 tablespoons UNSALTED BUTTER, softened, cut in ½-inch cubes**
- **12 tablespoons CREAM CHEESE, cut in ½-inch cubes**
- **1 teaspoon VANILLA EXTRACT**
- **1 tablespoon CRÈME FRAÎCHE**
- **1 to 2 teaspoons fresh LEMON JUICE**
- **3 to 4 tablespoons RHUBARB SYRUP (recipe follows)**
- **2 cups CONFECTIONER'S SUGAR, sifted**

1. Place the rhubarb, lemon juice, ginger, sugar, and water in a small saucepan. Bring the liquid to a boil over medium heat, stirring to dissolve the sugar.

2. Reduce the heat to low and simmer, stirring occasionally, for 10 minutes.

3. Remove the pan from the heat and allow the liquid to cool.

4. Strain out the rhubarb and ginger, reserving the syrup for the gob filling; press on the rhubarb pulp to extract as much color and flavor as possible. The syrup will keep in the fridge for 1 month.

FOR THE

RHUBARB SYRUP

2 cups coarsely chopped RHUBARB

JUICE of 1 LEMON

1 tablespoon peeled and chopped fresh GINGER

½ cup SUGAR

1 cup WATER

ORANGE, CRANBERRY, AND WALNUT GOBS

In the years before I hosted Thanksgiving dinner in my own house, I would make the drive from my apartment in Baltimore back to my folks' house in Pennsylvania for the holiday dinner. I always wanted to contribute something, but it had to be an item that could travel nearly four hours by car. So it became my tradition to bake very portable orange-cranberry muffins.

I'd arrive at my parents' home early on Thanksgiving morning, when the kitchen was warm and the fresh scent of the sautéed vegetables for the bird's stuffing still lingered in the room. We'd heat up the muffins I'd brought, and my parents would take a break from cooking. Sitting together at the kitchen table, we'd break open the muffins, slather them with butter, and share them over coffee.

These gobs are an adapted version of those muffins. They're perfect for Thanksgiving, but the hint of Grand Marnier helps take the chill out of any fall day.

1. Preheat the oven to 350°F. Line three 8-by-13-inch cookie sheets with parchment paper.

2. In a large bowl, sift together the flour, baking powder, baking soda, and salt. Whisk the dry ingredients until they're evenly distributed.

3. In another large bowl, cream the sugar and butter with a mixer on medium speed. Add the egg yolks to the creamed ingredients, and mix on medium. Then add the egg whites and vanilla, and mix on medium-high until the mixture looks like dense pudding. Add the cranberries and orange zest, and mix on high to incorporate them.

4. Alternate adding the dry ingredients and the buttermilk to the egg mixture, mixing on medium speed after each addition. Then add the sour cream and walnuts, and mix well.

5. Using a tablespoon or pastry bag, drop 1½-inch rounds of batter on the prepared cookie sheets, leaving 1 inch between each round. Bake them approximately 8 minutes, or until the gob domes have risen. Remove the gobs to a wire rack to cool.

FOR THE BATTER

- 4 cups all-purpose FLOUR
- ½ teaspoon BAKING POWDER
- 1½ teaspoons BAKING SODA
- 1 teaspoon SALT
- 2 cups SUGAR, sifted
- 8 tablespoons UNSALTED BUTTER, softened, cut in ½-inch cubes
- 2 EGGS, separated, at room temperature
- 1 teaspoon VANILLA EXTRACT
- ½ cup chopped fresh (or frozen) CRANBERRIES
- 1½ tablespoons ORANGE ZEST
- 1 cup BUTTERMILK, at room temperature
- 2 tablespoons SOUR CREAM
- ¼ cup finely chopped WALNUTS (preferably red walnuts)

1. Cream together the butter and cream cheese with a mixer on medium speed.

2. Add the vanilla, 1 tablespoon of lemon juice, 3 tablespoons of cranberry syrup, and the confectioners' sugar, and beat on medium-high speed until the mixture is fluffy; scrape the bowl with a spatula to reincorporate the ingredients if necessary. Taste and add another tablespoon of lemon juice if you like.

3. To frost the gobs, flip the baked gob domes over on a cookie sheet and match up pairs of similarly shaped domes. Add 1 tablespoon of filling to the flat side of an overturned dome, then place another dome on top, sandwich-style. Allow the gobs to fully set by refrigerating them on a baking sheet for at least 1 hour. Wrap the gobs in plastic wrap to prevent them from drying out.

FOR THE FILLING

- 8 tablespoons UNSALTED BUTTER, softened, cut in ½-inch cubes
- 12 tablespoons CREAM CHEESE, cut in ½-inch cubes
- 1 teaspoon VANILLA EXTRACT
- 1 to 2 tablespoons fresh LEMON JUICE
- 3 tablespoons CRANBERRY SYRUP (recipe follows)
- 2 cups CONFECTIONERS' SUGAR, sifted

1. Place the cranberries, ginger, cinnamon stick, cloves, sugar, and water in a small saucepan. Bring the liquid to a boil over medium heat, stirring to dissolve the sugar.

2. Reduce the heat to low and simmer, stirring occasionally, for 10 minutes.

3. Remove the pan from the heat, stir in the Grand Marnier and lemon juice, and and set it aside, covered, to let the syrup steep for at least 20 minutes.

4. Strain out the cranberries, ginger, cinnamon stick, and cloves, and reserve the syrup for the gob filling; press the pulp to extract as much liquid as possible. The syrup will keep in the fridge for 1 month.

FOR THE

CRANBERRY SYRUP

½ cup **CRANBERRIES, fresh or frozen (thawed)**

2 tablespoons peeled and coarsely chopped fresh **GINGER**

1 **CINNAMON STICK**

2 whole **CLOVES**

½ cup **SUGAR**

1 cup **WATER**

2 tablespoons **GRAND MARNIER**

JUICE of 1 **LEMON**

PERSIMMON AND MASCARPONE GOBS

RECIPE NO. 43

Say what you will about the various social-networking sites, but I owe the success of this gob to a Twitter post. I'd just bought several persimmons from the farmer's market, and they were chartreuse in color and hard as stone. I tried ripening these freshly picked tennis balls by putting them in a paper bag, but after forty-eight hours they hadn't softened a bit.

I tweeted a question, asking whether tossing an apple or a pear in the bag with the prematurely harvested fruits would help nudge them toward edibility—a common trick to hasten the ripening of other fruits. Within minutes I had several better suggestions. One of the most intriguing—from chef Patrick Colson of San Francisco's Café de la Presse—was to drip a bit of brandy into the calyx of each persimmon. Within two days, the alcohol-suckled persimmons had begun to turn their eponymous hue. Two days later they were soft, sweet, and aromatic. I was ready to bake my persimmon gobs.

RECIPE CONTINUES

1. Preheat the oven to 350°F. Line three 8-by-13-inch cookie sheets with parchment paper.

2. In a large bowl, sift together the flour, baking powder, baking soda, and salt. Whisk the dry ingredients until they're evenly distributed.

3. In another large bowl, cream the sugar and butter with a mixer on medium speed. Add the egg yolks to the creamed ingredients, and mix on medium. Then add the egg whites and vanilla, and mix on medium-high until the mixture looks like dense pudding. Add the persimmon pulp, and mix on high.

4. Alternate adding the dry ingredients and the buttermilk to the egg mixture, mixing on medium speed after each addition. Then add the sour cream, and mix well.

5. Using a tablespoon or pastry bag, drop 1½-inch rounds of batter on the prepared cookie sheets, leaving 1 inch between each round. Bake them approximately 8 minutes, or until the gob domes have risen. Remove the gobs to a wire rack to cool.

FOR THE BATTER

- 4 cups plus 2 tablespoons all-purpose FLOUR
- ½ teaspoon BAKING POWDER
- 1½ teaspoons BAKING SODA
- 1 teaspoon SALT
- 2 cups SUGAR, sifted
- 8 tablespoons UNSALTED BUTTER, softened, cut in ½-inch cubes
- 2 EGGS, separated, at room temperature
- 1 teaspoon VANILLA EXTRACT
- ½ cup PERSIMMON PULP (recipe follows)
- 1 cup BUTTERMILK, at room temperature
- 2 tablespoons SOUR CREAM

1. Cream the butter and mascarpone together with a mixer on medium speed until fluffy. Add the cream cheese, and mix again.

2. Add the vanilla, confectioners' sugar, 3 tablespoons of persimmon syrup, and 1 tablespoon of lemon juice, and beat until the mixture is fluffy; scrape the bowl with a spatula to reincorporate the ingredients if necessary. Taste and add another tablespoon of lemon juice or persimmon syrup if you like.

3. To frost the gobs, flip the baked gob domes over on a cookie sheet and match up pairs of similarly shaped domes. Add 1 tablespoon of filling to the flat side of an overturned dome, then place another dome on top, sandwich-style. Allow the gobs to fully set by refrigerating them on a baking sheet for at least 1 hour. Wrap the gobs in plastic wrap to prevent them from drying out.

FOR THE FILLING

- 8 tablespoons UNSALTED BUTTER, softened, cut in ½-inch cubes
- 8 tablespoons MASCARPONE
- 4 tablespoons CREAM CHEESE, cut in ½-inch cubes
- 1 teaspoon VANILLA EXTRACT
- 2 cups CONFECTIONERS' SUGAR, sifted
- 3 to 4 tablespoons PERSIMMON SYRUP (recipe follows)
- 1 to 2 tablespoons fresh LEMON JUICE

1. Wash the persimmons, and remove their calyxes (the leafy stems). Cut each persimmon in fourths. Use a grapefruit spoon or paring knife to remove the flesh from the peels, reserving both.

2. Put the persimmon flesh, vanilla bean and seeds, sugar, and water in small saucepan over medium heat, and stir until the sugar dissolves and the liquid comes to a simmer.

3. Add the persimmon peel and bring the liquid to a quick boil. Then reduce the heat to low and simmer, stirring occasionally, until the moisture has been cooked out and fruit becomes pulpy (about 10 minutes).

4. Remove the persimmon peel and vanilla bean. Stir in the lemon juice.

5. Remove the pan from the heat, setting aside, covered, to let the syrup steep for at least 20 minutes.

6. Strain the mixture to separate the pulp from the syrup, reserving the pulp for the gob batter and the syrup for the gob filling. Keep remaining persimmon pulp tightly covered in the fridge for one week.

FOR THE

PERSIMMON PULP AND SYRUP

2 cups peeled FUYU PERSIMMON, approximately four fruits

1 VANILLA BEAN, split, with seeds reserved

½ cup SUGAR

1 cup WATER

JUICE of 1 LEMON

KABOCHA
GARAM MASALA GOBS
WITH Orange Honey FILLING

Think of this as the international-fusion version of the Spiced Pumpkin Gob. The Japanese kabocha squash replaces the pumpkin—it's less sweet but still sturdy. And the usual pumpkin pie spices are replaced with the punchier garam masala spice blend.

I blend my own garam masala, purchasing and grinding all the spices individually. If you're buying a store-bought blend, make sure to read the label. Different regions of South Asia use very different blends, so look for mixes heavy on the star anise, clove, and cinnamon (and avoid those heavy on the peppers), which are the best complements to the sugar and honey.

NOTE: Since the kabocha will take about 45 minutes of prep time it is best to prepare that first. It can be done a day in advance and kept airtight in the fridge until ready to use.

1. Preheat the oven to 350°F. Line three 8-by-13-inch cookie sheets with parchment paper.

2. In a large bowl, sift together the flour, garam masala, baking powder, baking soda, and salt. Whisk the dry ingredients until they're evenly distributed.

3. In another large bowl, cream the sugar and butter with a mixer on medium speed. Add the egg yolks to the creamed ingredients, and mix on medium. Then add the egg whites and vanilla, and mix on medium-high until the mixture looks like dense pudding. Add the kabocha pulp, and mix on high.

4. Alternate adding the dry ingredients and the buttermilk to the egg mixture, mixing on medium speed after each addition. Then add the sour cream, and mix well.

5. Using a tablespoon or pastry bag, drop 1½-inch rounds of batter on the prepared cookie sheets, leaving 1 inch between each round. Bake them approximately 8 minutes, or until the gob domes have risen. Remove the gobs to a wire rack to cool.

---

1. Cream together the butter and cream cheese with a mixer on medium speed.

2. Add the vanilla, honey, orange juice, and confectioner's sugar, and beat on medium-high; scrape the bowl with a spatula to reincorporate the ingredients if necessary. Taste and add lemon juice to your liking.

3. To frost the gobs, flip the baked gob domes over on a cookie sheet and match up pairs of similarly shaped domes. Add 1 tablespoon of filling to the flat side of an overturned dome, then place another dome on top, sandwich-style. Allow the gobs to fully set by refrigerating them on a baking sheet for at least 1 hour. Wrap the gobs in plastic wrap to prevent them from drying out.

FOR THE BATTER

- 4 cups all-purpose **FLOUR**
- 2 tablespoons **GARAM MASALA**
- ½ teaspoon **BAKING POWDER**
- 1½ teaspoons **BAKING SODA**
- 1 teaspoon **SALT**
- 2 cups **SUGAR**, sifted
- 8 tablespoons **UNSALTED BUTTER**, softened, cut in ½-inch cubes
- 2 **EGGS**, separated, at room temperature
- 1 teaspoon **VANILLA EXTRACT**
- ½ cup **KABOCHA PULP** (recipe follows)
- 1 cup **BUTTERMILK**, at room temperature
- 2 tablespoons **SOUR CREAM**

FOR THE FILLING

- 8 tablespoons **UNSALTED BUTTER**, softened, cut in ½-inch cubes
- 12 tablespoons **CREAM CHEESE**, cut in ½-inch cubes
- 1 teaspoon **VANILLA EXTRACT**
- 2 tablespoons **ORANGE HONEY**
- 2 tablespoons fresh **ORANGE JUICE**
- 2 cups **CONFECTIONERS' SUGAR**, sifted
- 1 tablespoon fresh **LEMON JUICE** (optional)

1. Preheat the oven to 350°F. Prepare a greased baking sheet.

2. Peel the kabocha, cut it in half, and remove the seeds and stringy pulp. Then cut the squash into 1-inch cubes.

3. Place the kabocha cubes on the baking sheet, and scatter the garam masala over the squash. Put the kabocha in the oven and roast until it can be easily pierced with a fork (approximately 20 to 25 minutes).

4. Place the roasted kabocha in a saucepan with the brown sugar and water. Cook over medium heat, stirring occasionally to dissolve the sugar and further soften the kabocha. When pulp starts to form, after about 10 minutes, reduce the heat and stir in the lemon juice. Set aside and allow to cool.

5. Strain out the liquid, reserving the pulp for the gob batter. It should keep for one week, tightly covered, in the fridge.

FOR THE

KABOCHA PULP

1 medium **KABOCHA SQUASH** (about 3 pounds)

1 cup **WATER**

1 tablespoon **GARAM MASALA**

½ cup **BROWN SUGAR**

JUICE of 1 **LEMON**

VANILLA GOBS
WITH **QUINCE** FILLING

The first time I ate membrillo, I was smitten by its color and texture. It took me some time to realize that it's essentially the same thing as the quince paste that had been served to me on numerous cheese plates in my life. To make this beguiling spread, the apple-shaped, celery-hued quince is boiled down into a shimmering slab of rosy translucent paste.

When I first tried to make my own membrillo, I realized that quince syrup—an intermediate stage in the production of the paste—could also be used in a gob filling, with wonderful results.

I added quince to my vanilla gob recipe for a delicious pairing. A small bit of coriander was just enough to bring out the floral quality of the quince.

RECIPE CONTINUES

1. Preheat the oven to 350°F. Line three 8-by-13-inch baking sheets with parchment paper.

2. In a large bowl, sift together the flour, baking powder, baking soda, coriander, vanilla bean seeds, and salt. Whisk the dry ingredients until they're evenly distributed.

3. In another large bowl, cream the sugar and butter with a mixer on medium speed. Add the egg yolks to the creamed ingredients, and mix on medium. Then add the egg whites and vanilla, and mix on medium-high until the mixture looks like dense pudding. Add the quince pulp, and blend on high.

4. Alternate adding the dry ingredients and the buttermilk to the egg mixture, mixing on medium speed after each addition. Then add the sour cream, and mix well.

5. Using a tablespoon or pastry bag, drop 1½-inch rounds of batter on the prepared cookie sheets, leaving 1 inch between each round. Bake them approximately 8 minutes, or until the gob domes have risen. Remove the gobs to a wire rack to cool.

1. Cream together the butter and cream cheese with a mixer on medium speed.

2. Add vanilla, 1 tablespoon of lemon juice, quince syrup, and confectioners' sugar, and beat on medium-high; scrape the bowl with a spatula to reincorporate the ingredients if necessary. Taste and add another tablespoon of lemon juice if you like.

3. To frost the gobs, flip the baked gob domes over on a cookie sheet and match up pairs of similarly shaped domes. Add 1 tablespoon of filling to the flat side of an overturned dome, then place another dome on top, sandwich-style. Allow the gobs to fully set by refrigerating them on a baking sheet for at least 1 hour. Wrap the gobs in plastic wrap to prevent them from drying out.

FOR THE **BATTER**

- **4 cups plus 2 tablespoons all-purpose FLOUR**
- **½ teaspoon BAKING POWDER**
- **1½ teaspoons BAKING SODA**
- **1½ teaspoons GROUND CORIANDER**
- **1 VANILLA BEAN, pod split, seeds scraped and reserved**
- **1 teaspoon SALT**
- **2 cups SUGAR, sifted**
- **8 tablespoons UNSALTED BUTTER, softened, cut in ½-inch cubes**
- **2 EGGS, separated, at room temperature**
- **1 teaspoon VANILLA EXTRACT**
- **½ cup QUINCE PULP (recipe follows)**
- **1 cup BUTTERMILK, at room temperature**
- **2 tablespoons SOUR CREAM**

FOR THE **FILLING**

- **8 tablespoons UNSALTED BUTTER, softened, cut in ½-inch cubes**
- **12 tablespoons CREAM CHEESE, cut in ½-inch cubes**
- **1 teaspoon VANILLA EXTRACT**
- **1 to 2 tablespoons fresh LEMON JUICE**
- **3 tablespoons QUINCE SYRUP (recipe follows)**
- **2 cups CONFECTIONERS' SUGAR, sifted**

1. Wash the natural fuzz off the quince. Core the quince, remove the seeds, and coarsely chop the flesh with the skin on.

2. Place the quince, lemon juice, vanilla bean, sugar, and water in a saucepan. Bring the liquid to a boil over medium heat, stirring to dissolve the sugar.

3. Reduce the heat to low and simmer, stirring occasionally, until the quince pulp thickens and turns a reddish orange color (after about 20 minutes). Remove the pan from the heat and set it aside, covered, to let the syrup steep for at least 20 minutes

4. Remove the vanilla bean. Strain the quince pulp from the syrup, reserving the pulp for the gob batter and the syrup for the gob filling; press the pulp to extract as much liquid as possible.

FOR THE

QUINCE PULP AND SYRUP

2 cups QUINCE (about 4 to 5 large fruits)

JUICE of 1 LEMON

1 VANILLA BEAN left whole

½ cup SUGAR

1 cup WATER

COFFEE CARDAMOM GOBS

In my opinion, cardamom's aromatic qualities enhance every food and beverage that the spice infuses. It plays a major role in chai, but it does just as well when paired with coffee. Adding an equal amount of cocoa powder always makes everything better! A dollop of crème fraîche in the filling keeps things interesting.

1. Preheat the oven to 350°F. Line three 8-by-13-inch baking sheets with parchment paper.

2. In a large bowl, sift together the flour, cardamom, cocoa powder, espresso powder, baking powder, baking soda, and salt. Whisk the dry ingredients until they're evenly distributed.

3. In another large bowl, cream the sugar and butter with a mixer on medium speed. Add the egg yolks to the creamed ingredients, and mix on medium. Then add the egg whites and vanilla, and mix on medium-high until the mixture looks like dense pudding.

4. Alternate adding the dry ingredients and the buttermilk to the egg mixture, mixing on medium speed after each addition. Then add the sour cream, and mix well.

5. Using a tablespoon or pastry bag, drop 1½-inch rounds of batter on the prepared cookie sheets, leaving 1 inch between each round. Bake them approximately 8 minutes, or until the gob domes have risen. Remove the gobs to a wire rack to cool.

FOR THE **BATTER**

- 4 cups plus 2 tablespoon all-purpose FLOUR
- 2 tablespoons GROUND CARDAMOM
- 2 tablespoons COCOA POWDER, such as Green & Black's organic
- 2 tablespoons ESPRESSO POWDER, such as King Arthur's
- ½ teaspoon BAKING POWDER
- 1½ teaspoons BAKING SODA
- 1 teaspoon SALT
- 2 cups SUGAR, sifted
- 8 tablespoons UNSALTED BUTTER, softened, cut in ½-inch cubes
- 2 EGGS, separated, at room temperature
- 1 teaspoon VANILLA EXTRACT
- 1 cup BUTTERMILK, at room temperature
- 2 tablespoons SOUR CREAM

1. Cream together the butter and cream cheese with a mixer on medium speed.

2. Add the vanilla, 1 tablespoon of lemon juice, the crème fraîche, and the confectioners' sugar, and beat on medium-high; scrape the bowl with a spatula to reincorporate the ingredients if necessary. Taste and add another tablespoon of lemon juice if you like.

3. To frost the gobs, flip the baked gob domes over on a cookie sheet and match up pairs of similarly shaped domes. Add 1 tablespoon of filling to the flat side of an overturned dome, then place another dome on top, sandwich-style. Allow the gobs to fully set by refrigerating them on a baking sheet for at least 1 hour. Wrap the gobs in plastic wrap to prevent them from drying out.

FOR THE **FILLING**

- 8 tablespoons UNSALTED BUTTER, softened, cut in ½-inch cubes
- 12 tablespoons CREAM CHEESE, cut in ½-inch cubes
- 1 to 2 tablespoons VANILLA EXTRACT
- 1 to 2 tablespoons fresh LEMON JUICE
- 2 tablespoons CRÈME FRAÎCHE
- 2 cups CONFECTIONERS' SUGAR, sifted

VANILLA LAVENDER
GOBS WITH Blackberry FILLING

I started experimenting with making a lavender gob when I was growing the purple-sprigged herb in my backyard. I strongly urge you to use fresh lavender in this recipe if you can get it. Dried lavender is fine in a pinch, but do not overuse it. Its aromatic properties can turn your gobs into something akin to bars of scented soap, at least in terms of their overpowering fragrance. The blackberries in the filling's syrup will add a feisty edge to help balance the lavender and will also help deepen the filling's purplish hue.

1. Preheat the oven to 350°F. Line three 8-by-13-inch baking sheets with parchment paper.

2. In a large bowl, sift together the flour, baking powder, baking soda, and salt. Whisk the dry ingredients until they're evenly distributed.

3. In another large bowl, cream the sugar and butter with a mixer on medium speed. Add the egg yolks to the creamed ingredients, and mix on medium. Then add the egg whites and vanilla, and mix on medium-high until the mixture looks like dense pudding. Add the lavender, and mix on medium-high.

4. Alternate adding the dry ingredients and the buttermilk to the egg mixture, mixing on medium speed after each addition. Then add the sour cream, and mix well.

5. Using a tablespoon or pastry bag, drop 1½-inch rounds of batter on the prepared cookie sheets, leaving 1 inch between each round. Bake them approximately 8 minutes, or until the gob domes have risen. Remove the gobs to a wire rack to cool.

FOR THE **BATTER**

- 4 cups plus 2 tablespoons all-purpose FLOUR
- ½ teaspoon BAKING POWDER
- 1½ teaspoons BAKING SODA
- 1 teaspoon SALT
- 2 cups SUGAR, sifted
- 8 tablespoons UNSALTED BUTTER, softened, cut in ½-inch cubes
- 2 EGGS, separated, at room temperature
- 1 teaspoon VANILLA EXTRACT
- 1 tablespoon fresh LAVENDER SEEDS, finely chopped, or 1½ teaspoons dried
- 1 cup BUTTERMILK, at room temperature
- 2 tablespoons SOUR CREAM

1. Cream the butter and cream cheese together with a mixer on medium speed until they're fluffy.

2. Add the vanilla, vanilla bean seeds, 1 tablespoon of lime juice, the lavender-blackberry syrup, and the confectioners' sugar, and beat on medium-high speed; scrape the bowl with a spatula to reincorporate the ingredients if necessary. Taste and add another tablespoon of lime juice if you like.

3. To frost the gobs, flip the baked gob domes over on a cookie sheet and match up pairs of similarly shaped domes. Add 1 tablespoon of filling to the flat side of an overturned dome, then place another dome on top, sandwich-style. Allow the gobs to fully set by refrigerating them on a baking sheet for at least 1 hour. Wrap the gobs in plastic wrap to prevent them from drying out.

FOR THE **FILLING**

- 8 tablespoons UNSALTED BUTTER, softened, cut in ½-inch cubes
- 12 tablespoons CREAM CHEESE, cut in ½-inch cubes
- 1 VANILLA BEAN, split, with seeds scraped and reserved
- 1 to 2 tablespoons fresh LIME JUICE
- 3 tablespoons LAVENDER-BLACKBERRY SYRUP (recipe follows)
- 2 cups CONFECTIONERS' SUGAR, sifted

1. Place the blackberries, lavender, vanilla, sugar, and water in a saucepan. Bring the liquid to a boil over medium heat, stirring to dissolve the sugar.

2. Reduce the heat to low and simmer, stirring occasionally, until the mixture becomes a rich purple color and the lavender is aromatic (at least 10 minutes).

3. Remove the pan from the heat, stir in the lemon juice, and set it aside, covered, to let the syrup steep for at least 20 minutes.

4. Remove the lavender sprigs, if using. Strain out the solids and reserve the syrup for the gob filling. Syrup will keep, tightly covered in the fridge, for up to two weeks.

FOR THE

LEMON-BLACKBERRY SYRUP

- ½ cup **BLACKBERRIES**
- 1 teaspoon dried **LAVENDER SEEDS** or 2 or 3 fresh lavender sprigs
- 1 teaspoon **VANILLA EXTRACT**
- ½ cup **SUGAR**
- ½ cup **WATER**
- 1 tablespoon **LEMON JUICE**

S'MORE GOBS

I kicked around the idea of creating a s'more gob for a while, but I thought simply selling the finished gobs would take all the fun out of the campfire treat. Serving them at a dinner party, with some assembly at the table, was an idea that hearkened back to Russel and Mary Wright's 1950 classic, *Guide to Easier Living*, in which they suggested that dinner guests be invited to participate in the meal's preparation. It also seemed like a good way to preserve some of the Wrights' do-it-yourself spirit. In this tableside version, a brûlée torch stands in for the open-pit fire.

There's a little game-day preparation involved in this recipe, but the rest can be done in advance. Bake the gob domes ahead of time and store them, wrapped, so they stay moist. If the chocolate is chopped and ready to melt, you can whip up the glaçage and filling while the dinner dishes are being cleared. Bring the gobs to the table and pass the filling so guests can build their own dessert. When every guest has a healthy dollop of filling on the flat side of one gob, it's time to pass the torch. Let everyone caramelize the peaks of the icing for a toasted-marshmallow effect. Instruct the guests to place another gob dome on top of the frosted one. Then pass the chocolate glaçage to ladle over the gobs.

RECIPE CONTINUES

1. Preheat the oven to 350°F. Line three 8-by-13-inch baking sheets with parchment paper.

2. In a large bowl, sift together the flour, cocoa powder, cinnamon, baking powder, baking soda, and salt. Add the graham cracker crumbs, and whisk the dry ingredients until they're evenly distributed.

3. In another large bowl, cream the sugar and butter with a mixer on medium speed. Add the egg yolks to the creamed ingredients, and mix on medium. Then add the egg whites and vanilla, and mix on medium-high until the mixture looks like dense pudding.

4. Alternate adding the dry ingredients and the buttermilk to the egg mixture, mixing on medium speed after each addition. Then add the sour cream, and mix well.

5. Using a tablespoon or pastry bag, drop 1½-inch rounds of batter on the prepared cookie sheets, leaving 1 inch between each round. Bake them approximately 8 minutes, or until the gob domes have risen. Remove the gobs to a wire rack to cool.

FOR THE BATTER

- 3½ cups all-purpose FLOUR
- ½ cup COCOA POWDER
- 1 tablespoon CINNAMON
- ½ teaspoon BAKING POWDER
- 1½ teaspoons BAKING SODA
- 1 teaspoon SALT
- ½ cup finely crumbled GRAHAM CRACKERS
- 2 cups SUGAR, sifted
- 8 tablespoons UNSALTED BUTTER, softened, cut in ½-inch cubes
- 2 EGGS, separated, at room temperature
- 1 teaspoon VANILLA EXTRACT
- 1 cup BUTTERMILK, at room temperature
- 2 tablespoons SOUR CREAM

1. Whisk the egg whites, sugar, and cream of tartar in heat proof bowl over pan of simmering water until the sugar is dissolved and the ingredients are warm, not hot.

2. Immediately transfer the mixture to a mixing bowl, and whip it on low, then medium, then medium-high speed until peaks begin to form.

3. Slowly drizzle the vanilla into the bowl and mix until it's incorporated and the peaks are stiff.

4. To assemble the gobs, add 1 tablespoon of filling to the flat side of an overturned dome. Pass a brûlée torch over the filling to "toast" it. Then place another gob dome on top. Drizzle the chocolate glaçage (recipe follows) over the top of the gobs.

FOR THE FILLING

- 8 EGG WHITES, at room temperature
- 2 cups GRANULATED SUGAR, sifted
- ½ teaspoon CREAM OF TARTAR
- 2 teaspoons VANILLA EXTRACT

1. Place the chocolate pieces in a heat-resistant bowl.

2. Heat the heavy cream over medium heat until it comes to a boil. Immediately pour the cream over the chocolate pieces and stir quickly to evenly melt the chocolate.

3. Add 2 tablespoons of butter to the bowl and stir until it's evenly distributed. Take a ladle, scoop up some of mixture, and drizzle it back into the bowl. If it doesn't stream easily, quickly add another tablespoon of butter. Be careful to incorporate all butter so it doesn't leave any telltale streaks of white and yellow in your glaçage.

FOR THE

GLAÇAGE

- 6 ounces **SEMI SWEET CHOCOLATE** (preferably Green & Black's organic), chopped in ¼-inch pieces
- ¾ cup **HEAVY CREAM**
- 2 to 3 tablespoons **UNSALTED BUTTER**, in small squares

PEAR AND STAR ANISE
GOBS WITH ALMOND FILLING

On my visits to San Francisco, prior to moving here, I would take the bus out to the Asian grocery stores on Clement Street and load up on spices that I couldn't easily get back east at the time. I was particularly fond of the big bags of star anise. The spice looks like something carefully carved from tiny pieces of wood. Its very essence—its shape, its aroma, its unique flavor—made me think of it as a small treasure.

Each time I returned to my East Coast kitchen with a new bag, I would excitedly make a big pot of pho, the anise lending an exotic licorice fragrance to the soup. But I'd never baked with it before, and when my first batch of Pear and Star Anise Gobs came out of the oven, they were long overdue.

You can choose between Western pears or Asian pears for this recipe. The former are more delicate in flavor, so I recommend removing the whole star anise from the pot about halfway through the simmering, so they don't overpower the pear in the filling.

1. Preheat the oven to 350°F. Line three 8-by-13-inch baking sheets with parchment paper.

2. In a large bowl, sift together the flour, baking powder, baking soda, and salt. Whisk the dry ingredients until they're evenly distributed.

3. In another large bowl, cream the sugar and butter with a mixer on medium speed. Add the egg yolks to the creamed ingredients, and mix on medium. Then add the egg whites and vanilla, and mix on medium-high until the mixture looks like dense pudding. Add the pear pulp, and blend on medium-high.

4. Alternate adding the dry ingredients and the buttermilk to the egg mixture, mixing on medium speed after each addition. Then add the sour cream, and mix well.

5. Using a tablespoon or pastry bag, drop 1½-inch rounds of batter on the prepared cookie sheets, leaving 1 inch between each round. Bake them approximately 8 minutes, or until the gob domes have risen. Remove the gobs to a wire rack to cool.

1. Cream together the butter and cream cheese with a mixer on medium speed. Add the grated almond paste. Mix well.

2. Add the vanilla, almond extract, 1 tablespoon of lemon juice, 3 tablespoons of pear syrup, and the confectioners' sugar, and beat on medium-high speed; scrape the bowl with a spatula to reincorporate the ingredients if necessary. Taste and add another tablespoon of lemon juice or pear syrup if you like.

3. To frost the gobs, flip the baked gob domes over on a cookie sheet and match up pairs of similarly shaped domes. Add 1 tablespoon of filling to the flat side of an overturned dome, then place another dome on top, sandwich-style. Allow the gobs to fully set by refrigerating them on a baking sheet for at least 1 hour. Wrap the gobs in plastic wrap to prevent them from drying out.

FOR THE BATTER

- 4 cups plus 2 tablespoons all-purpose FLOUR
- ½ teaspoon BAKING POWDER
- 1½ teaspoons BAKING SODA
- 1 teaspoon SALT
- 2 cups SUGAR, sifted
- 8 tablespoons UNSALTED BUTTER, softened, cut in ½-inch cubes
- 2 EGGS, separated, at room temperature
- 1 teaspoon VANILLA EXTRACT
- ½ cup PEAR PULP (recipe follows)
- 1 cup BUTTERMILK, at room temperature
- 2 tablespoons SOUR CREAM

FOR THE FILLING

- 8 tablespoons UNSALTED BUTTER, softened, cut in ½-inch cubes
- 8 tablespoons CREAM CHEESE, cut in ½-inch cubes
- ½ cup GRATED ALMOND PASTE
- ½ teaspoon VANILLA EXTRACT
- ½ teaspoon ALMOND EXTRACT
- 1 to 2 tablespoons fresh LEMON JUICE
- 3 to 4 tablespoons PEAR SYRUP (recipe follows)
- 2 cups CONFECTIONERS' SUGAR, sifted

1. Put the chopped pears, star anise, sugar, and water in a saucepan. Bring the liquid to a boil over medium heat, stirring to dissolve the sugar.

2. Reduce the heat to low and simmer, stirring occasionally, until the pear mixture reduces by half (about 20 minutes). If you're using a Western pear variety, remove the star anise after about 10 minutes. If you're using an Asian pear variety, remove the star anise after the mixture has been reduced.

3. Remove the pan from heat, stir in the lemon juice, and set it aside, covered, to let the syrup steep for at least 20 minutes.

4. Strain the pulp from the syrup, reserving the pulp for the gob batter and the syrup for the gob filling. If the pear pulp seems too thick and is more of a glob than a smooth pulp, quickly pulse it in a food processor.

FOR THE

PEAR PULP AND SYRUP

4 PEARS, peeled, cored, and coarsely chopped

2 whole **STAR ANISE**

½ **cup SUGAR**

1 cup WATER

JUICE of 1 LEMON

PLUM, RUM, GINGER GOBS

If ever there was a dessert with a redundant name, it's the plum tart. More times than I can count, I have ordered one expecting the sweet lusciousness of a chin-drenching ripe plum and instead have bitten into a pucker-inducing forkful of tartness.

The plums in this recipe are coaxed into a sweeter state thanks to the addition of rum and brown sugar.

RECIPE CONTINUES

1. Preheat the oven to 350°F. Line three 8-by-13-inch baking sheets with parchment paper.

2. In a large bowl, sift together the flour, baking powder, baking soda, and salt. Add the crystallized ginger. Whisk the dry ingredients until they're evenly distributed.

3. In another large bowl, cream the sugar and butter with a mixer on medium speed. Add the egg yolks to the creamed ingredients, and mix on medium. Then add the egg whites and vanilla, and mix on medium-high until the mixture looks like dense pudding. Add the plum pulp, and blend on medium-high.

4. Alternate adding the dry ingredients and the buttermilk to the egg mixture, mixing on medium speed after each addition. Then add the sour cream, and mix well.

5. Using a tablespoon or pastry bag, drop 1½-inch rounds of batter on the prepared cookie sheets, leaving 1 inch between each round. Bake them approximately 8 minutes, or until the gob domes have risen. Remove the gobs to a wire rack to cool.

FOR THE BATTER

- **4 cups plus 2 tablespoons all-purpose FLOUR**
- **½ teaspoon BAKING POWDER**
- **1½ teaspoons BAKING SODA**
- **1 teaspoon SALT**
- **2 tablespoons CRYSTALLIZED GINGER, pulverized**
- **2 cups minus 2 tablespoons SUGAR, sifted**
- **8 tablespoons UNSALTED BUTTER, softened, cut in ½-inch cubes**
- **2 EGGS, separated, at room temperature**
- **1 teaspoon VANILLA EXTRACT**
- **½ cup PLUM PULP (recipe follows)**
- **1 cup BUTTERMILK, at room temperature**
- **2 tablespoons SOUR CREAM**

1. Cream together the butter and cream cheese with a mixer on medium speed.

2. Add the vanilla, 1 tablespoon of lemon juice, 3 tablespoons of plum syrup, and the confectioners' sugar, and beat on medium-high; scrape the bowl with a spatula to reincorporate the ingredients if necessary. Taste and add another tablespoon of lemon juice or plum syrup if you like.

3. To frost the gobs, flip the baked gob domes over on a cookie sheet and match up pairs of similarly shaped domes. Add 1 tablespoon of filling to the flat side of an overturned dome, then place another dome on top, sandwich-style. Allow the gobs to fully set by refrigerating them on a baking sheet for at least 1 hour. Wrap the gobs in plastic wrap to prevent them from drying out.

FOR THE FILLING

- **8 tablespoons UNSALTED BUTTER, softened, cut in ½- inch cubes**
- **12 tablespoons CREAM CHEESE, cut in ½-inch cubes**
- **1 teaspoon VANILLA EXTRACT**
- **1 to 2 tablespoons fresh LEMON JUICE**
- **3 to 4 tablespoons PLUM SYRUP (recipe follows)**
- **2 cups CONFECTIONERS' SUGAR, sifted**

1. Place the plums, ginger, brown sugar, rum, and water in a medium saucepan. Bring the liquid to a boil over medium heat, stirring to dissolve the sugar.

2. Reduce the heat to low and simmer, stirring occasionally, until the plum mixture reduces by half (approximately 20 minutes).

3. Remove the pan from the heat and stir in the lemon juice. Set the syrup aside, covered, to steep for at least 20 minutes.

4. Strain the pulp from the syrup, reserving the pulp for the gob batter and the syrup for the gob filling. Remove the ginger pieces from the pulp. If the plum skins have cooked off, remove the skins from pulp. If they haven't, pulse it through a food processor for a few minutes to incorporate them. Plum mixture will keep, tightly covered, in the fridge for a week

FOR THE
PLUM PULP AND SYRUP

- 6 large **PLUMS**, pits removed
- 1 tablespoon fresh **GINGER**, sliced into 5 or 6 coin-shaped pieces
- 1 cup **BROWN SUGAR**
- 2 tablespoons **DARK RUM**
- ½ cup **WATER**
- **JUICE of 1 LEMON**

PEANUT BUTTER GOBS

The peanut butter cookies that I ate as a kid spoiled me. The singular characteristic of my grandmother's and my mom's peanut butter cookies was their wonderful moistness. Their cookies were gently pliable and chewy, the fork print atop each one creating a latticework in the soft batter.

After growing up with such exemplary treats, I, to my great dismay, have encountered more than my share of bad peanut butter cookies over the years—cookies so dry as to be brittle or even sandy. I learned to shun most peanut butter–flavored confections, not willing to risk the disappointment.

These gobs brought me back into the light. The secret: bacon fat! Not only does it make this gob magically moist; it also heightens the savory quality of the peanut butter, which balances the sweetness.

NOTE: A little clarified bacon fat goes a long way, but you can adjust this recipe according to your palate. I suggest starting with a single tablespoon of bacon fat in the gob batter, but you can substitute additional bacon fat for the butter if you wish—up to four tablespoons total—without compromising its consistency.

1. Preheat the oven to 350°F. Line three 8-by-13-inch baking sheets with parchment paper.

2. In a large bowl, sift together the flour, baking powder, baking soda, and salt. Whisk the dry ingredients until they're evenly distributed.

3. In another large bowl, cream the sugar, butter, and bacon fat. Add the egg yolks to the creamed ingredients, and mix on medium. Then add the egg whites and vanilla, and mix on medium-high until the mixture looks like dense pudding. Add the peanut butter, and blend on medium-high until it's well incorporated.

4. Alternate adding the dry ingredients and the buttermilk to the egg mixture, mixing on medium speed after each addition. Then add the sour cream, and mix well.

5. Using a tablespoon or pastry bag, drop 1 ½-inch rounds of batter on the prepared cookie sheets, leaving 1 inch between each round. Bake them approximately 8 minutes, or until the gob domes have risen. Remove the gobs to a wire rack to cool.

FOR THE BATTER

- 4 cups plus 2 tablespoons all-purpose FLOUR
- ½ teaspoon BAKING POWDER
- 1½ teaspoons BAKING SODA
- 1 teaspoon SALT
- 2 cups SUGAR, sifted
- 7 tablespoons UNSALTED BUTTER, softened, cut in ½-inch cubes
- 1 tablespoon BACON FAT, rendered from approximately 3 slices
- 2 EGGS, separated, at room temperature
- 1 teaspoon VANILLA EXTRACT
- ½ cup good-quality smooth PEANUT BUTTER
- 1 cup BUTTERMILK, at room temperature
- 2 tablespoons SOUR CREAM

1. Cream together the butter and cream cheese with a mixer on medium speed.

2. Add the vanilla, 1 tablespoon of lemon juice, and confectioners' sugar, and beat on medium-high speed; scrape the bowl with a spatula to reincorporate the ingredients if necessary. Taste and add another tablespoon of lemon juice if you like.

3. To frost the gobs, flip the baked gob domes over on a cookie sheet and match up pairs of similarly shaped domes. Add 1 tablespoon of filling to the flat side of an overturned dome, then place another dome on top, sandwich-style. Allow the gobs to fully set by refrigerating them on a baking sheet for at least 1 hour. Wrap the gobs in plastic wrap to prevent them from drying out.

FOR THE FILLING

- 8 tablespoons UNSALTED BUTTER, softened, cut in ½- inch cubes
- 12 tablespoons CREAM CHEESE, cut in ½-inch cubes
- 2 tablespoons plus 1 teaspoon VANILLA EXTRACT
- 1 to 2 tablespoons fresh LEMON JUICE
- 2 cups CONFECTIONERS' SUGAR, sifted

GINGERBREAD
GOBS

Depending on how many of the recipes you've read and/or made in this book, you have probably deduced, somewhat correctly, that almost anything can be baked into a gob. With some slight adjustments for leavening, volume, and acidity, nearly any flavor combination and ingredient you can think of can get gobbed. That's another reason why I was so drawn to this confection when I first started baking them. The way my parents and my grandparents cooked, nothing went to waste, because quite honestly, nothing could.

Even now, in my shared commercial kitchen space, when I have a tablespoon or two of grated ginger, orange zest, or fresh lemon juice left over, I will walk around asking whether any of the other chefs or caterers might be able to make use of it.

The recipes and histories behind classic gingerbread seem to suggest a similar use-what-you-have approach, as if someone were emptying out what remained in the entire spice bin. A little more cinnamon in this batch, a little less allspice in the next.

So, when making this gob, adjust the nutmeg, ground clove, cinnamon, or allspice measurements to your liking. Add a few tablespoons of finely chopped walnuts, grated orange, or rum-soaked raisins to the batter if you prefer. Dust the finished gobs with confectioners' sugar or drizzle them with a milk-and-sugar glaze.

1. Preheat the oven to 350°F. Line three 8-by-13-inch baking sheets with parchment paper.

2. In a large bowl, sift together the flour, ginger, cinnamon, allspice, nutmeg, baking powder, baking soda, and salt. Whisk the dry ingredients until they're evenly distributed.

3. In another large bowl, cream the sugar and butter with a mixer on medium speed. Add the egg yolks to the creamed ingredients, and mix on medium. Then add the egg whites and vanilla, and mix on medium-high until the mixture looks like dense pudding. Add the raisins, if using, and mix until they're thoroughly distributed.

4. Alternate adding the dry ingredients and the buttermilk to the egg mixture, mixing on medium speed after each addition. Then add the sour cream, and mix well.

5. Using a tablespoon or pastry bag, drop 1½-inch rounds of batter on the prepared cookie sheets, leaving 1 inch between each round. Bake them approximately 8 minutes, or until the gob domes have risen. Remove the gobs to a wire rack to cool.

1. Cream together the butter and cream cheese with a mixer on medium speed.

2. Add the vanilla, 1 tablespoon of lemon juice, and the confectioners' sugar, and beat on medium-high; scrape the bowl with a spatula to reincorporate the ingredients if necessary. Taste and add another tablespoon of lemon juice if you like.

3. To frost the gobs, flip the baked gob domes over on a cookie sheet and match up pairs of similarly shaped domes. Add 1 tablespoon of filling to the flat side of an overturned dome, then place another dome on top, sandwich-style. Allow the gobs to fully set by refrigerating them on a baking sheet for at least 1 hour. You can lightly dust them with confectioners' sugar, or even a light sprinkling of sea salt, before serving. Wrap the gobs in plastic wrap to prevent them from drying out.

FOR THE BATTER

- 4 cups plus 2 tablespoons all-purpose FLOUR
- 2 tablespoons GROUND GINGER
- 1 tablespoon CINNAMON
- 1 teaspoon ground ALLSPICE
- 1 teaspoon ground NUTMEG
- ½ teaspoon BAKING POWDER
- 1½ teaspoons BAKING SODA
- 1 teaspoon SALT
- 2 cups SUGAR, sifted
- 8 tablespoons UNSALTED BUTTER, softened, cut in ½-inch cubes
- 2 EGGS, separated, at room temperature
- 1 teaspoon VANILLA EXTRACT
- ½ cup GOLDEN RUM-SOAKED RAISINS (optional; recipe follows)
- 1 cup BUTTERMILK, at room temperature

FOR THE FILLING

- 8 tablespoons UNSALTED BUTTER, softened, cut in ½- inch cubes
- 12 tablespoons CREAM CHEESE, cut in ½-inch cubes
- 2 tablespoons VANILLA EXTRACT
- 1 to 2 tablespoons fresh LEMON JUICE
- 2 cups CONFECTIONERS' SUGAR, sifted

1. Place the raisins, rum, brown sugar, and lemon juice in small saucepan. Heat the mixture over medium heat, stirring occasionally, until it's heated through and the sugar has dissolved.

2. Remove the pan from the heat. Strain raisins, pressing to remove excess liquids.

3. Transfer the mixture to a food processor, and coarsely chop on the pulse setting.

FOR THE

RUM-SOAKED RAISINS

1 cup **GOLDEN RAISINS**
1 tablespoon **LIGHT RUM**
1 teaspoon **LIGHT BROWN SUGAR**
JUICE of ½ **LEMON**

ACKNOWLEDGMENTS

Gobs of Thanks. This book was written, in large part, because of the help, encouragement and inspiration I received from many people. While I can't list everyone that purchased gobs from me, or that provided words of praise through emails, Twitter tweets, and blog posts, please know I am grateful for your support.

I'd like to thank the bakers of all the gobs that I ate as a kid growing up in Pennsylvania. Even though I never met most of you, the products of your kitchens helped establish my own "taste of home." Also, a sincere thanks to the good people of San Francisco and Oakland for being so welcoming of an odd-named confection you'd never heard of and for being so nice to the guy who baked them.

A special thank you goes out to the vendors who sold and continue to sell their wares from carts and trucks and folding tables and even brown paper bags on sidewalks and street corners. You inspire me and give me courage. I respect you all.

And a personal thank you to the following. Please know any omission was not intentional. Kelly Potchak, Gary and Jennifer Witt, Adams Hussey & Associates, San Francisco; Adams Hussey & Associates Washington, D.C., Olivia Ongpin, Anthony Quintal, Brian Frank, Murat and Pelin Celebi, Kristin Hoppe, Natalie Glazier, Logan Mitchell, John Birdsall, Virginia Miller, Marcia Gagliardi,

Karen Gore, Lisa Church, Heather Lunan, Luis and Monica Licea, Martin Meeker, Scott Lietzke, Ed Chui, Jason Rotairo, Mandy Harper, Ben Hebel, Roger Feely, Desiree Solomon, Dontaye Ball, Caleb Zigas and La Cocina, Matt Cohen and Off the Grid, Eclectic Cookery, CUESA, Eat Real Festival, Anya Fernald, Shari Hansen, Susan Coss, Hedy McFarren, Shakirah Simley, Paawan Kothari, Broke Ass Stuart, Anthony Myint, Richie Nakano, Kitty Gallisa, Joey Alhearne, Namu, Senor Sisig, Eric Rud, Gillian Shaw, Doug Williams, Pal's Takeaway, Avedano's, Jonathan Ward, Mark Livosky, Patric Yumul, Donovan Unks, David Dunn, Donna Hall, Catherine Bergstrom, Trina de Joya, Debi Shawcross, John T. Edge, Tiffany Lam, Alex Rando, Jon Clark, Abraham Despiritu, Alison Okabayashi, Jeff Krupman, Dottie Guy, Amihan Crisostome, Eileen Hassi and Ritual Roasters, Sightglass, Lisette Titre, Patrick Colson, Cameo Wood, Jun Belen, Kate Kuckro, Mindy Canner, Dynamo Donuts, Humphry Slocombe, Kung Fu Tacos, Peter Perez, Chronicle Books, the *San Francisco Chronicle*, Sara Adler, Lynne Bennett, Stacy Finz, Google, Twitter, Levi's, Square, 18 Reasons, the Commonwealth Club, Brian Kimball, Christian Ciscle, Emily Olson, Rob LaFave, Christina Olson, every one at Foodzie, *SFoodie*, *SF Weekly*, Cesalee Farr, Ryan Farr, Ryan Sarver, Devon Biondi, Bill Horst, Brett Yost, the Yost family, Kurt B. Reighley, Jim and Cammiel Hussey, Keri Maijala, Tamara Palmer, Nate Knaebel, Maureen Klier, Rachel Mannheimer, Sara Mercurio, Kathy Belden, Dave Dunton, Harvey Klinger Agency, Bloomsbury Publishing, the Ramones, Curtis and Sara Kimball, Amy Chapman and family, Seth Chapman and family, Margo Demark, Sam Zannino, Larry and Rachel Hirsch, Amy and Ian Foor, David and Vicky Potchak, Terri Potchak and family, Mark Gdula and family, Judi MacIntyre and family, the Gobsters, and Lon Chapman. Lastly I extend my immeasurable and eternal gratitude to my parents, Peter and Helen Gdula.

INDEX

A NOTE ON THE AUTHOR

Steven Gdula was born in Cambria Country, Pennsylvania, and raised on gobs. His writing has appeared in *Details*, the *Washington Post, Time Out,* the *Advocate, Cooking Light,* and elsewhere, and he is the author of *The Warmest Room in the House,* a social history of the American kitchen. He is the proprietor of Gobba Gobba Hey in San Francisco, and he blogs at thewarmestroominthehouse.blogspot.com and gobbagobbahey.com.